GRAND CANYON
NATIONAL PARK

**Photography
by
Michael D. Yandell**

Michael D. Yandell,
Publisher and Editor in Chief
Constance R. Yandell,
Editor
Edward R. Yandell
Managing Editor

Cartographer, Norton Allen

Special Historical Consultant, Otis "Dock" Marston

Lithography by Graphic Arts Division of World-Wide Research and Publishing Company

TABLE OF CONTENTS

National Parkways, A Photographic and Comprehensive Guide to Grand Canyon National Park, is published by the National Parks Division of World-Wide Research and Publishing Company, 2000 Zero Road, Casper, Wyoming 82601. Copyright© 1977 by World-Wide Research and Publishing Company. All rights reserved.

Front Cover — The view northwest from Grandview Point.

Inside Front Cover — Deer Creek Falls.

Inside Back Cover — Crimson flowers of the ocotilla arch gracefully over this view of the Colorado River and Grand Canyon two miles below Diamond Creek.

Back Cover — Near Pima Point, the graceful sweep of weathered wood provides foreground to an otherwise rugged scene of spires and buttes characteristic of the mid-western regions of the Grand Canyon.

This Page — The Datil Yucca has been an important plant to the Indians of the Southwest.
Soap was derived from its roots; its leaves and fibrous parts were woven into baskets, clothing and rope, and its fruit provided nourishment.

"The Grand Canon fills me with awe.
It is beyond comparison—beyond description;
absolutely unparalleled throughout the wide world . . . .
Let this great wonder of nature remain as it now is.
Do nothing to mar its grandeur, sublimity and loveliness.
You cannot improve on it.
But what you can do is to keep it for your children,
your children's children, and all who come after you,
as the one great sight which every American should see . . . .
Don't let them skin this wonderful country—as they will try to do."
Theodore Roosevelt, May 6, 1903.

THE GRAND CANYON

Horrid Abyss, Wondrous Titan of Chasms

Text

by

John F. Hoffman

Edited

by

World-Wide Research

INTRODUCTION

The Grand Canyon is one of the outstanding natural wonders of planet Earth. For many, few experiences equal their first view of the expansive chasm, a vista which evokes marvel at the extraordinary and magnificent landscape and wonder at its meaning and significance. Many canyon visitors would agree with J. Cecil Alter who, fifty years ago, made the observation, "To me the Grand Canyon stands apart as one of life's greater episodes," and with the sentiment expressed by John L. Stoddard in 1898, "To stand upon the edge of this stupendous gorge, as it receives its earliest greeting from the god of day, is to enjoy in a moment compensation for long years of ordinary uneventful life."

The scenic beauty and intangible values of the Grand Canyon, however, were not always appreciated. The contemporary concept of beauty and worth in natural landscapes was not always part of the aesthetic value of Western Civilization. Rugged and harsh landscapes were once thought worthless. Only lands altered by the development of man, cultural landscapes, were admired.

Isolation of the Grand Canyon, its precipitous cliffs, awesome depths and the dangerous rapid plagued Colorado River contributed to an impression of severity and forbiddance. Many early visitors found the canyon ominous.

The first Europeans to observe the massive Grand Canyon, a Spanish exploring expedition led by Garcia Lopez de Cardenas in 1540, considered the great chasm austere and an obstacle to travel.

Man's aesthetic attitude toward wild lands began to change when a new artistic and literary movement, Romanticism, developed in Europe during the late Eighteenth Century. The transition between the old attitude of the worthlessness of wilderness and a new appreciation for their intrinsic values was gradual. Perception of the Grand Canyon reflected this changing attitude and impressions often expressed values of both attitudes. Views of early canyon explorers demonstrate this dualism.

In 1858, while commanding an exploring expedition to the canyon, Army Lieutenant Joseph Christmas Ives described the country as a "profitless locality," but he also said it presented "a splendid panorama" and was a "wondering delight".

A member of the expedition, F. W. von Egloffstein, made the first sketches of the Grand Canyon which he portrayed with exaggerated vertical walls, crowded close together, shrouded in darkness.

Eleven years later, a former Civil War Union Army officer, Major John Wesley Powell, led the first boat expedition through the Grand Canyon. Powell referred to the "black depths" of the chasm, although he also called it "the most sublime spectacle on the earth" and wrote that "the glories and the beauties of form, color, and sound unite in the Grand Canyon."

The appreciation of wilderness beauty grew through the Nineteenth Century, but many people still viewed rugged natural landscapes as ugly and perilous.

The Grand Canyon was abhorrent to the Reverend C. B. Spencer who wrote it was "Horror! Tragedy! Silence! Death! Chaos! There is the awful canyon in five words." He also condemned the canyon as "the delirium of Nature." In a similar tone, C. S. Gleed said it was "the grave of the world."

In contrast, the redoubtable Southwest enthusiast, Charles Fletcher Lummis perceived the Grand Canyon as "the greatest thing in the world," and William E. Curtis wrote "it is impossible to exaggerate the grandeur, the sublimity, the impressiveness of the scenery." Canyon visitor Fred W. Parker characterized the abyss as "that summation of all grandeur" and to C. A. Higgins it was simply, but impressively, "the titan of chasms."

In 1906, Theodore Roosevelt illustrated how far the appreciation of beauty in wilderness had developed when he spoke at the Grand Canyon and said of the spectacular chasm, "leave it as it is. You cannot improve upon it. The ages have been at work upon it, and man can only mar it."

Such impressions demonstrated the impact the emergence of Romanticism had on perception of natural landscapes, the realization and appreciation of beauty in undeveloped lands, the wilderness. Man's concept of beauty and the value of untamed landscapes had greatly changed and a significant legacy was the preservation of the Grand Canyon of the Colorado River.

MAN IN THE DESERT WILDERNESS
A Human History
of the
Colorado River and its Grand Canyon

The Ancient People of the Colorado Plateau.

When man first encountered and occupied the Grand Canyon region is not definitely known, but archaeological evidence suggests that people of the Desert Culture were probably the earliest inhabitants and had descended into the depths of the spectacular chasm between 3500 to 4000 years ago.

Desert Culture people were prehistoric North American Indians that inhabited the Intermontane area of western North America between approximately 6000 to 2000 B.C. They followed a primitive hunting and gathering way of life in which they collected their subsistence directly from the environment without the benefit of agriculture. They were nomadic and probably lived in small kin related groups.

People of the Desert Culture apparently entered the Grand Canyon at infrequent intervals. Evidence of their presence in the canyon has been found in caves of the prominent Redwall Limestone cliffs where they left animal figurines. These remarkable artifacts were made of split willow twigs, some pierced by small spears, and suggest the Desert Culture people used them in a hunting ceremony. The age of one of these split-twig figurines was determined by radiocarbon dating to be 2145 B.C. plus or minus 100 years.

Approximately 2000 years passed between the placing of the unique split-twig figurines in the Redwall caves and evidence of a new or different prehistoric habitation of the Grand Canyon country. These new people were the Anasazi and the Cohonina.

The Anasazi Indians, who were probably descendants of the Desert Culture people, are well known for their ruins in Mesa Verde National Park and Canyon de Chelly National Monument. The Grand Canyon was on the western border of the Anasazi territory and was occupied for a period of about 600 years from A.D. 600 to 1200.

The Anasazi inhabited both the North and South Rims and also lived within the canyon. Two hundred and seventy three Anasazi sites have been located in the Walhalla Glades near Cape Royal on the North Rim while the Tusayan ruin on the South Rim is but one of more than 100 Anasazi sites near the south side of the canyon. Although there are several sites of Anasazi habitation within the canyon, an area of particular interest lies along the 20-mile stretch of the Colorado River between Nankoweap Creek, in the lower end of the Marble Gorge, and Unkar Creek. South of the mouth of Nankoweap Creek, about 500 feet up the west canyon wall, are several Anasazi masonry grain storage structures.

Because of their practice of agriculture, the Anasazi were able to develop a more prosperous culture than their ancestors had experienced and they were able to live a more settled community oriented life.

The Anasazi abandoned the Grand Canyon country by A.D. 1200. Their leaving was probably the result of a combination of reasons rather than one specific problem. Among the reasons may have been drouth, an influx of hostile Indians and exhaustion of natural resources.

The Cohonina Indians were contemporary with the Anasazi. They lived south of the Grand Canyon and west of the Anasazi during the period from about A.D. 700 to 1200. Their greatest population density was attained between 900 and 1100 and they traded with the neighboring Anasazi. One of the Grand Canyon areas occupied by the Cohonina was Havasu Canyon, a southeast tributary in the western part of the great chasm. Beginning about A.D. 1100 and continuing for perhaps one hundred years, the Indians concentrated in Havasu Canyon. This trend was probably due to the same reasons that caused the Anasazi to abandon the Grand Canyon area. By about 1150, the Cohonina were essentially limited to Havasu Canyon. One theory suggest that the present canyon dwellers, the Havasupai Indians, are their descendants. Another theory holds that the Havasupai are descended from Pai Indians, "The People," who displaced the Cohonina from the Grand Canyon country about A.D. 1150. These Pai, according to this theory, were also the ancestors of the present Hualapai, or Walapai, "pine tree folk," who live to the west of the Havasupai and south of the Colorado River.

The story of Indian occupation of the canyon and its surrounding area was a tale of adaptation to a difficult environment, but this adaptation did not conflict with the natural or rugged beauty of the region. The trend was for the Indian to exist in harmony with the land for the land was his home. His religion was natural, based primarily upon deities and ceremonies concerning hunting and agriculture, but by the early 1500's events were taking place which would cloud and finally destroy much of the Indian way of life in the Southwest. Spain had entered the New World and her quest for gold as well as her missionary zeal would inexorably lead members of her expeditionary forces to invade Indian land of the American Southwest. As a consequence the Spanish would be the first Europeans to discover the Colorado River and its magnificent Grand Canyon.

The Conquering Spanish;
an Era of Soldiers, Priests and Discovery.

In 1528, Panfilo de Narvaez, governor of Spanish Florida, commanded an expedition which was to explore much of the western coast of the Florida Peninsula. Narvaez divided his expeditionary forces into two groups, one under his leadership, went inland, the second remained aboard ships which were to rendezvous with the land personnel at a later date.

The land party's travel was slow and plagued by a lack of food and attacks by Indians. More than three months after separating from the ships, Narvaez and his party reached St. Andrew Bay, but the ships had been missed and would not be seen again.

In the hope of reaching Mexico, the stranded men constructed five crude boats and set sail on a westward course along the Gulf coastline. Eventually the boats separated, some of the men were lost at sea while others made shore.

Nearly eight and one half years later, in March, 1536, four members of the ill-fated expedition encountered Spaniards on the Rio Sinaloa in western Mexico. The four lost men were Alvar Nunez Cabeza de Vaca, Andres Dorantes de Carranca, Alonzo del Castillo Maldonado and a black slave named Esteban. They had struggled along the Texas gulf coast into parts of the American Southwest and through northern Mexico during their incredible odyssey. With the weary quartet came a story about great Indian cities with fabulous wealth which lie to the north of Mexico.

This story was of great interest to Antonio de Mendoza, the Viceroy of New Spain, for a legend with its roots in the Mohammedan Moors of the Eighth Century, said somewhere were seven great cities of fabulous wealth. Possibly the cities related in the story of the lost men were the rich cities celebrated by legend.

In the spring of 1539, the Viceroy sent Esteban and Fray Marcos de Niza to locate the cities. Esteban traveled ahead of the priest and posed as a black god before the Indians. He reported to Fray Marcos that the area through which they were traveling was known to the Indians as Cibola, and that name became attached to the cities of legendary wealth. Esteban traveled through southern Arizona and into west central New Mexico arriving at the Zuni Indian pueblo of Hawikuh where the pretending deity was supposedly murdered by the Indians. Fray Marcos, who was traveling some distance behind Esteban, saw the pueblo from afar, however, he never entered or made a close examination of the adobe city. When Fray Marcos returned to Mexico he fallaciously reported that he had actually seen one of the legendary cities of great golden wealth.

Shortly after Mendoza had sent Fray Marcos and Esteban north, he ordered Francisco de Ulloa to sail three ships up the coast into the Gulf of California. Ulloa departed from Acapulco on July 8, 1539, and eventually reached the head of the gulf on September 27, 1539. In so doing, Ulloa established that Baja California was a peninsula and not an island as had been thought. The ships were anchored and Ulloa took possession of the surrounding country in the name of the King of Spain. He could not find any evidence of human occupation and wrote, "I do not believe that such a land can be inhabited." He also named the reddish colored sea the Ancon de San Andres y Mar Bermejo "because it is that color and we arrived there on St. Andrews Day."

Although the mouth of the Colorado River was observed from the ships, Ulloa apparently did not go up the river or give it a name. Ulloa's expedition made two important discoveries. They were the first recorded Europeans to see the Colorado River and they established that California was not an island.

Viceroy Mendoza sent two more expeditions in search of the golden cities of legend. Francisco Vasquez de Coronado was given command of a large land expedition which was supplemented by a military escort under the direction of Melchior Diaz. The second expedition was to go by sea. It was placed under the leadership of Hernando de Alarcon and was to sail up the Gulf of California with supplies for Coronado's expedition.

Coronado marched north and on July 7, 1540 found the Zuni pueblo of Hawikuh where Esteban had been killed. However, the city proved to be constructed only of stone and adobe mortar. Its streets were not paved with gold and there were no riches to be had.

The Alarcon expedition reached the mouth of the Colorado River on August 26, 1540 and Alarcon was the first European to give the Colorado River a name, the first of several bestowed on it by white men. He named the river, El Rio de Buena Guia, or "The River of Good Guidance."

At the mouth of the Colorado, Alarcon and his crew transferred to small boats and proceeded up river an unknown distance, making Alarcon and his crew the first European navigators of the Colorado River.

When local Indians informed Alarcon that Coronado had reached Hawikuh, Alarcon decided to return to Mexico. Before he departed, a cross was erected, some letters buried, and a sign placed which read, "Alarcon came this far. There are letters at the foot of this tree."

In late September, Melchior Diaz, with a party of twenty five men set off to find Alarcon and the supply ships. Diaz came to a great river which he called the Rio del Tison, the "Firebrand River," because the local Indians carried firebrands to warm their bodies. This was the second name given to the Colorado by white men. The Indians informed Diaz that Alarcon had been in the area and the letters were found. Diaz and his party crossed the Colorado on rafts and explored some of the nearby country before returning to Mexico.

In the intervening time, Coronado learned of a pueblo group to the west called Tusayan, the Hopi pueblos, and in July of 1540, dispatched Pedro de Tovar and a party of soldiers to locate these pueblos. Upon reaching Tusayan, Tovar learned of Indians, probably the Havasupai, living near a large river to the west. However, since he was not under orders to proceed beyond Tusayan, Tovar returned to Coronado.

In August, Coronado sent Garcia Lopez de Cardenas to find the river of which Tovar had heard. From Tusayan, Indians guided Cardenas' party through desert country and after a march of twenty days they reached the South Rim of the Grand Canyon, becoming the first Spaniards to view the canyon and the fourth group to see the Colorado River. These events occurred in late September, 1540, only forty eight years after Columbus' first voyage to the new world. At what point on the South Rim Cardenas' expedition first saw the canyon is unknown and it has not been established if Cardenas gave the chasm a name.

Cardenas and his men spent three days searching along the rim for some way to descend to the river. Finally, three members of the expedition, Pablos de Melgosa, Juan Galeras, and an unidentified companion, attempted to make a descent. After having gone about one-third of the way to the river the trio decided to turn back. They reached the rim around four o'clock of the same day of their descent and expressed great surprise at the size of many of the rocks which, from the rim, had not appeared so large. They stated that what looked to be easy hiking and short distances were not so. Instead, the canyon was vast and difficult to travel. These three men hold the distinction of being the first Spaniards to hike and climb in the Grand Canyon.

After four days of exploring the canyon's South Rim, a shortage of water caused Cardenas to curtail his activities and he set off to rejoin Coronado. The Grand Canyon had been discovered, but with the departure of Cardenas it was not to be again observed by Spaniards for nearly two hundred and fifty years.

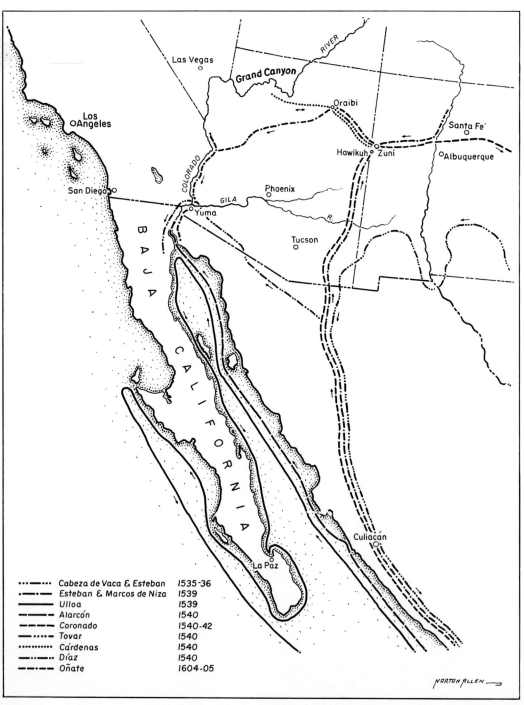

••••••	Cabeza de Vaca & Esteban	1535-36
•—•—	Esteban & Marcos de Niza	1539
————	Ulloa	1539
——————	Alarcón	1540
————	Coronado	1540-42
—•••••	Tovar	1540
••••••••	Cardenas	1540
—••—••—	Díaz	1540
—•—•—	Oñate	1604-05

NORTON ALLEN

Below Grandview Point, the river meanders through a "grand" and ancient museum of natural history.

From Mile 134 where Tapeats Creek joins the Colorado River.

The next major event associated with the Grand Canyon's master carver, the Colorado River, occurred in 1604 when Juan de Onate, the Spanish governor of the province of New Mexico, organized an expedition to journey to the Pacific Coast where he hoped to find wealth in oyster pearls. Onate's party consisted of thirty men and two priests. One of the priests was Fray Francisco de Escobar, who wrote a chronicle of the journey.

Part of their route was along the Bill Williams River in Arizona to its junction with the Colorado. Fray Escobar recorded that the Colorado was named the "Rio de Buena Esperanza, because we reached it on the day of the expectation or hope of the most happy parturition of the Virgin Mary, our Lady." Rio de Buena Esperanza, or River of Good Hope, was the third name assigned to the Colorado by the Spanish.

Onate moved his expedition south along the Colorado to its mouth at the Gulf of California, but the hoped for riches from oyster pearls never materialized.

Nearly one hundred years were to elapse before the next momentous events on the Colorado River. These events involved a remarkable, historic figure, the Jesuit priest, Eusebio Francisco Kino. Fray Kino spent twenty-four years in the area of southern Arizona and Mexico's northern Sonora. Between 1687 and 1711, the year of his death, Kino made over fifty trips through the region and founded many missions. He personally performed some five thousand Indian baptisms.

In 1539, Francisco de Ulloa found California was a peninsula, but the results of his historic voyage were not generally known or accepted. Thus, on November 3, 1701, Fray Kino, with a small expedition, set forth from Mission Dolores on the Altar River in Sonora to determine if California was an island or a peninsula. If California was a peninsula, Kino hoped to locate a land route to the territory. They traveled northwest across an arid landscape toward the Colorado River. The expedition crossed the Colorado approximately thirty miles below its junction with the Gila River and continued westward from the Colorado to an Indian village where Kino learned the Pacific Ocean could be reached in a 10 days walk to the west, and the Gulf of California was only a one day walk to the south. Kino had re-discovered that California was not an island and that it could be reached by a land route. He did not go farther west, but returned to Sonora.

At Mission Dolores he prepared a significant map. On this map, which showed California as a peninsula, he gave the Colorado River its present name. Colorado in Spanish means red. The name apparently came from the commonly reddish color of the river's water. Occasionally the name has been anglicized to Red River.

In 1774, Juan Bautista de Anza, captain of the presidio at Tubac, organized an expedition to establish a land supply route to California. He set out on January 8 and successfully reached Mission San Gabriel in California thus opening the land passage that Kino had determined nearly 75 years earlier.

Anza returned to Tubac, where he began a second expedition on October 23, 1775, to Mission San Gabriel and, ultimately, to found San Francisco in 1776. Fray Francisco Tomas Garces, a Franciscan missionary at Mission San Xavier del Bac, near Tucson, accompanied Anza to the junction of the Colorado and Gila Rivers. He remained at the Yuma Indian villages for a time and explored the surrounding country. On February 14, 1776, Garces departed to seek a land route between New Mexico and California. Accompanied on his

Even though this is a desert climate with summer temperatures exceeding 100°F, spring brings a momentary mantle of greenery to the inner canyon.

journey by Indians, the party proceeded up the Colorado and reached the Mojave Indian villages above present day Needles, California where Garces visited with the Indians and left on March 4.

Garces crossed the Colorado and made an excursion into California to Mission San Gabriel, which he reached on March 24. From there, he continued northward to the San Joaquin Valley, then south-eastwardly to the Colorado River. Crossing the river, he entered present day Arizona. Garces encountered a group of Havasupai Indians who requested that the priest accompany them to their village in the bottom of Havasu Canyon, also called Cataract Canyon, a southern branch of the Grand Canyon. Garces wrote that in order to reach the Havasupai village he "traversed a strait" and that "on one side is a very lofty cliff, and on the other a horrible abyss." Once past this place "there presented itself another and worse one." Here Garces left his mule so that he "might climb down a ladder of wood." He reached the floor of the canyon and Havasupai village on June 20, 1776. The priest saw the canyon home of the Indians and witnessed their way of life.

Garces stayed with the Havasupai through June 24. The next day, accompanied by five Indians, he ascended a precipitous canyon wall to the surface of the Coconino Plateau and traveled several miles over the plateau. Garces wrote that on the following day, June 26, "I traveled four leagues southeast, and south, and turning to the east; and halted at the sight of the most profound caxones which ever onward continue; and within these flows the Rio Colorado. There is seen a very great sierra, which in the distance (looks) blue; and there runs from southeast to northwest a pass open to the very base, as if the sierra were cut artificially to give entrance to the Rio Colorado into these lands."

The view west
at Point Sublime.

Dark Vishnu schist,
fluted by erosion
and intruded with lighter colored granite
dates from the earliest period of geologic history
exposed in the walls of the Grand Canyon.

Flat topped Wotans Throne as it appears
from the end of the foot trail at Cape Royal on the North Rim.

The Grand Canyon of the Colorado River
is an expression of natural sculpture unique in grandeur and scale,
and while the canyon has no need of mankind,
mankind may have a fundamental
need to experience yet preserve those qualities
which make this place such a wondrous delight.

Pages 18 and 19.
Conquistador Isle near Mile 121 of the Grand Canyon.
This section of the canyon is known for its extended exposure
of nearly horizontal layers of Tapeats Sandstone which form
the lower walls of this lengthy corridor.

In a few places,
canyon walls are so steep that they eclipse
sunlight from the river and its banks
for all but a few hours near noon.

Spectacular Navajo Falls in Havasu Canyon
is located a short distance below Havasu Village and only a few hundred yards
above famed Havasu Falls. This fall, like those below it,
is enhanced by dense foliage which parts to reveal stately travertine formations
which seem to cascade like falling water down the sheer face of the cliff.

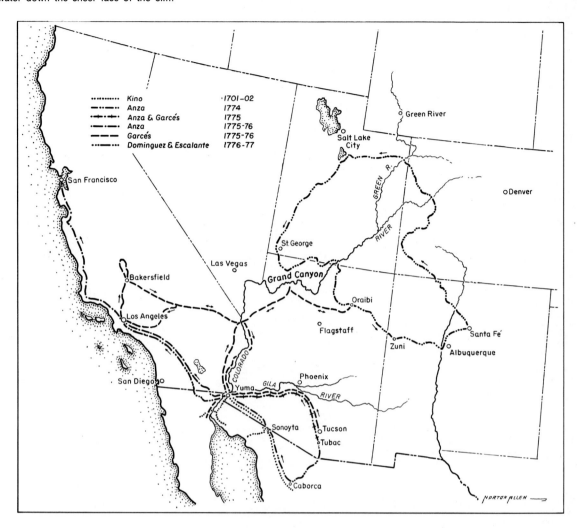

Although Garces said the canyon lay to the east-northeast from his viewpoint, there can be little certainty as to the actual location from which he viewed the canyon. In any case, as a consequence of his travels, Garces had become, on June 26, 1776, the first European in nearly two hundred and fifty years to again see the Grand Canyon of the Colorado River.

The Spanish priest was the first white man of record to name the canyon. He called it Puerto de Bucareli, or Bucareli Pass, a pass to the Colorado River. The name was given in honor of the Viceroy of New Spain, Antonio Maria Bucareli y Ursua.

After re-discovering the Grand Canyon, Garces journeyed easterly to Oraibi, one of the Tusayan, or Hopi, pueblos. The Hopi were unfriendly and he returned to the home of the Havasupai. Garces arrived there on July 6, 1776 and remained with the Havasupai for six days. He then set out on the return trip to Mission San Xavier del Bac, where his adventure of discovery and re-discovery ended on September 17, 1776.

In the same year that Fray Garces visited the Havasupai and saw the Grand Canyon, two Franciscan friars, Francisco Atanasio Dominguez and Silvestre Velez de Escalante, mounted an expedition to find a better overland trail to California than Anza's route. They set out from Santa Fe, New Mexico on July 29, 1776. After several months of difficult travel they turned back short of their objective.

On October 16, 1776, they encountered Indians. Escalante recorded the meeting in his diary. "We stopped and talked with them more than two and a half or three hours. They told us that in two days we would reach the Rio Grande (Colorado), but would not be able to go the way we wanted to, because there was no watering place, nor would we be able to cross the river in this region because it ran through a great canyon and was very deep and had on both sides extremely high cliffs and rocks, and finally, that from here to the river the terrain was very bad."

The "great canyon" the Indians warned about was the Grand Canyon. The explorers, not deterred, continued toward the Colorado and reached the great river on October 26. They camped near the future site of Lee's Ferry, at the head of the Grand Canyon, but were unable to ford the river. They named the place in frustration, but with humor, San Benito Salsipuedes, or "San Benito Get-Out-If-You-Can."

The expedition remained at camp for six days and on November 2 departed in search of a crossing. Finally, on November 7, in Glen Canyon, thirty-nine miles upriver from Lee's Ferry, they were able to cross the river at a place they named La Purisima Concepcion de la Virgen Santisima, but today called El Vado de los Padres, or "The Crossing of the Fathers." The sight of the crossing is now submerged beneath Lake Powell. At about five o'clock in the afternoon, when the entire expedition had safely reached the opposite side of the river, Escalante recorded they celebrated by "praising God our Lord and firing off a few muskets as a sign of the great joy which we all felt at having overcome so great a difficulty and which had caused us so much labor and delay."

From the river, they continued their homeward journey reaching Santa Fe on January 2, 1777.

The Dominguez-Escalante expedition made several historic findings. They discovered the principal tributary to the Colorado River, the Green River; they were the first Europeans to reach the site of Lee's Ferry; and the first to see and cross magnificent Glen Canyon.

In 1821, Mexico gained independence from Spain. The nation's northern territory encompassed most of the vast Colorado River drainage region including the Grand Canyon. Spain had barred foreign merchants from its territory, but now Mexico would allow them entrance. Consequently, traders from the United States visited northern Mexican settlements and American fur trappers expanded their search for beaver into the area.

Sometimes wild,
sometimes quiet,
the river flows on beneath the majestic
limestone walls of the Marble Gorge.

James Ohio Pattie
and the "Horrid Mountains."

The first Americans to see the Grand Canyon were probably members of a fur trapping expedition. In early 1826, James Ohio Pattie joined a party of French-American trappers "bound for Red River." On March 28, after several harrowing and bloody encounters with the Indians of the area, Pattie reported that the trapping party "reached a point of the river where the mountains shut in so close upon its shores, that we were compelled to climb a mountain, and travel along the acclivity, the river still in sight, and at an immense depth beneath us. Through this whole distance, which we judged to be, as the river meanders, 100 leagues, we had snow from a foot to eighteen inches deep. The river bluffs on the opposite shore, were never more than a mile from us. It is perhaps, this very long and formidable range of mountains, which has caused, that this country of Red River, has not been more explored, at least by the American people."

The trappers moved along the chasm's rim for thirteen days and on April 10, according to Pattie, they "arrived where the river emerges from these horrid mountains, which so cage it up, as to deprive all human beings of the ability to descend to its banks, and make use of its waters. No mortal has the power of describing the pleasure I felt, when I could once more reach the banks of the river."

If this journey actually did occur, it was an odyssey of incredible dimensions. However, the accuracy of Pattie's account of his travels may be impossible to determine for dates and routes seem suspect and the recounting of his adventures are embellished with exaggeration.

Pattie's "acclivity" has frequently been identified as the Grand Canyon. If it was, this 1826 trip might be the first American visit to the canyon; however, the description of the acclivity does not seem to properly fit the Grand Canyon topography. Pattie stated that the canyon was never more than a mile wide. Although this statement can be applied to the upper narrow Marble Gorge of the canyon, it is generally untrue for other parts of the canyon's length where widths of over ten miles are found.

In the fall of 1827, George C. Yount led a trapping party from Taos to the lower Colorado River. It is reported that Yount's party descended to the bottom of the Grand Canyon. If they did, these trappers, in 1828, may have been the first white men to achieve that singular honor.

23

The declivity of the inner gorge
from Toroweap Point.

The United States Gains the Grand Canyon.

In 1846, the United States and Mexico went to war. The Mexican War was the result of several problems, among them the Manifest Destiny and expansionist policies of the United States, disputes over the status of Texas and boundary disagreements. The United States defeated Mexico and the Treaty of Guadalupe Hidalgo was signed on February 2, 1848. In losing the war, Mexico ceded a large tract of its northern territory to the United States. Within this vast territory was the beautiful Grand Canyon country and almost the full length of the Colorado River.

Following the accession of this new territory, the government of the United States conducted several expeditions to examine the country. One of these early explorations was under the command of Army Captain Lorenzo Sitgreaves who, in 1851, explored stretches of the Little Colorado and the lower Colorado River, but never saw the Grand Canyon.

The California gold rush of 1849 attracted thousands of miners to the gold fields and the Gila Trail which followed the Gila River westward to its junction with the Colorado River near present day Yuma, Arizona was one of the routes used for several years by the gold seekers. In 1850, a ferry was established at the Colorado River crossing. Later that same year, Camp Independence, a U. S. Army fortification, was established to protect the ferry from Indian harassment. In 1852 the installation was moved and renamed Fort Yuma.

The army decided to supply the fort by a water route rather than over the arid and difficult terrain from San Diego, a region which was characterized by Captain Rufus Ingalls as "the worst and most irksome desert for beasts in the world."

Early Navigation, Steamboats on the Lower Colorado.

Lieutenant George Horatio Derby was ordered to examine the navigability of the Colorado from its mouth at the head of the Gulf of California to Fort Yuma. Upon completion of his survey, Derby prepared a map of the river and reported that the Colorado River "may be navigated at any season of the year by a steamboat of eighteen or twenty feet beam, drawing two and a half to three feet water." This favorable report led to the development of steam navigation on the lower Colorado River.

In 1851, George Alonzo Johnson secured a contract to supply Fort Yuma with provisions and in early 1852 he attempted to sail a supply laden schooner upriver to Yuma, but was unable to reach the fort. He subsequently transferred the provisions to two 50-foot by 18-foot flatboats which were poled upriver, but the venture was far from successful and Johnson was unable to satisfactorily supply the fort by flatboats.

A new contract was given to James Turnbull who obtained a sixty-five foot long side-wheel steamboat, the *Uncle Sam,* to transport supplies to the fort. This was the first steamer on the Colorado. It reached Fort Yuma on December 3, 1852, requiring fifteen days to travel approximately 120 miles upriver from the mouth of the Colorado. The pioneer steamer made several more voyages to Yuma, but when it sank in 1853 Turnbull abandoned his steamboat effort.

Early the next year, Johnson put a side-wheel steamer, the *General Jesup,* into operation. The vessel was 104 feet long with a beam of seventeen feet and was powered by a seventy horsepower engine. A year later he added another steamboat, the 120-footer *Colorado.* Other steamers were to follow and provide transportation along the lower Colorado.

Early Proposals to Explore the Grand Canyon.

In 1853, Lieutenant Randolph Barnes Marcy proposed that he conduct an exploration of the canyon by "taking small rowboats and ascending the river from the debouche of the gorge at a low stage of water." He wanted to go upriver rather than down because as he said, "there would be no danger of being carried over dangerous rapids or falls, and the boats could be carried around difficult passages."

He stated further that "Such an exploration could not, in my judgment, prove otherwise than intensely interesting, as the scenery here must surpass in grandeur any other in the universe." But the Lieutenant had another reason to explore the canyon. He wanted to search its walls for gold and silver.

These precious metals had been found east and west of the canyon and Marcy reasoned, "Is it not, therefore, probable that the walls of this gigantic crevice will exhibit many rich deposits?" He also posed the enticing question, "who knows but that the government might here find a source of revenue sufficient to liquidate our national debt?"

Lieutenant Marcy did not make the anticipated exploration and prospecting trip in the canyon. Ironically, his proposal was denied due to a lack of available federal funds.

Another hopeful explorer of the Grand Canyon was reported to be John Wise. He proposed a novel method of exploration, the use of a balloon. Wise, a pioneer American balloonist, sought funds from Congress for the aerial reconnaissance, but was unsuccessful.

In 1856, George Johnson requested funds from the federal government to determine the lower Colorado's head of navigation. Secretary of War Jefferson Davis, later President of the Confederate States of America, was persuaded to include the river survey in the War Department's budget request to Congress. When the budget, which included $70,000.00 for the Colorado River survey was approved, Johnson mistakenly assumed he would be given the funds and he began to make plans for the survey.

The Ives Expedition.

At this same time, the Federal Territorial Government of Utah faced a hostile Mormon environment and the Army was ordered to send a force to solidify Federal authority; however, supply routes had to be established for operations in Utah as well as other posts in the West. Because the Colorado River offered a possible route, Army Lieutenant Joseph Christmas Ives was directed to ascertain how far steamboats could navigate upriver. He was additionally appointed to examine the river and its tributaries in the vicinity of the Grand Canyon.

To test the river, Ives secured a steamboat, the *Explorer,* which was built in Philadelphia by Reaney, Neafie & Co. The vessel was fifty-four feet long, had an iron hull, stern-wheel and was equipped with a four-pound howitzer for armament. After trial runs on the Delaware River, the steamer was dismantled, shipped to the mouth of the Colorado, and reassembled.

Subsequently, George Johnson learned of the Ives expedition. Wanting to be the first to find the head of steamer navigation on the Colorado, Johnson hurriedly mounted a private expedition. He applied to the Commander of Fort Yuma for a military escort. Lieutenant James L. White was ordered to take fifteen of his soldiers and accompany Johnson.

On December 31, 1857, Johnson and his party left Yuma aboard the *General Jesup.* They steamed upriver about 200 miles, or approximately 325 miles above the mouth of the river. At this point, Lieutenant White reported "we found a succession of three rapids, which would have required a day for us to overcome." They transferred to a small boat and continued about five miles upriver. White stated "the extreme point reached by us was about 35° 18' Latitude and about fifty miles in Longitude west of Fort Yuma." This location is about fifty-five miles below present Hoover Dam and is now under the waters of Lake Mohave. Unable to continue farther, Johnson turned the bow of the *General Jesup* downriver and began the voyage back to Yuma.

"BIG CANON AT MOUTH OF DIAMOND RIVER"
is from a sketch made by F. W. Egloffstein,
an artist and topographer who was a member of the 1856 expedition
led by Army Lieutenant Joseph Christmas Ives
which had been assigned the task of determining the head of steamer navigation
on the lower Colorado River and to investigate the Grand Canyon or Big Canon
as it was then called. This sketch and its companion
on the opposite page are noteworthy for their exaggerated view of the canyon
although they may give some insight as to the feelings of the explorers
and the anxiety they felt upon their descending into the place.
Lieutenant Ives wrote,
"the corresponding depth and gloom of the gaping chasms
into which we were plunging, imparted an earthly character
to a way that might have resembled the portals of the infernal regions.
Harsh screams issuing from aerial recesses in the canon sides
and apparitions of goblin-like figures perched in the rifts and hollows
of the impending cliffs, gave an odd reality to this impression."
For a more accurate picture of the canyon
near the mouth of the Diamond River see the inside back cover.

Lieutenant Ives began his upriver expedition from the mouth of the Colorado on December 31, 1857, the same day Johnson embarked from Yuma. Thus, Ives was approximately 125 miles behind Johnson. The *Explorer* started on its historic voyage with, Ives noted in his report, "a shrill scream from the whistle." Because of shoals and sandbars, travel was slow and difficult. After a few days, Ives left the steamer and proceeded ahead to Yuma, part of the distance in a skiff and the remainder by horse.

At Yuma, Ives joined additional members of his expedition that had come overland from San Diego and from Fort Tejon to meet the *Explorer*. Among those at Yuma were Dr. John Strong Newberry, the expedition's physician and geologist; Balduin Mollhausen, a Prussian artist; and F. W. von Egloffstein, the topographer and artist.

The steamer reached Yuma on January 9 and two days later started upriver with twenty-seven on board. The going was not always pleasant as shallow water, snags, and sandbars repeatedly presented themselves and hindered progress. A letter written by Dr. Newberry described his view of life aboard the *Explorer*: "Day after day as we slowly crawl along up the muddy Colorado—confined to a little tucked up over-loaded, over-crowded steamer with no retreat from the cold, heat, wind or drifting sand, and nothing but the monotony of an absolute desert to feast our eyes upon, with nothing but bacon and beans and rice and bread *and sand*—or rather *sand and bacon*, etc., to eat, sleeping on shore on a sand drift, eyes, nose, mouth, ears, clothes and bed filled with sand—with almost everyone discontented and cross."

On the 30th of January, nineteen days from Yuma, and about five miles below present Parker, Arizona, the little Army steamer met Johnson and his party aboard the *General Jesup* which was on its return voyage to Yuma. The two steamers stopped and Ives learned about upriver conditions.

On March 6, 1858, after almost two months travel, the *Explorer* struck a submerged rock near the mouth of Black Canyon in which Hoover Dam is now located. The spot is about twenty-one miles below the dam and approximately thirty-five miles above the upriver mark attained by George Johnson.

Ives described the collision with the rock. "The *Explorer*, with a stunning crash, brought up abruptly and instantaneously against a sunken rock. For a second the impression was that the canon had fallen in. The concussion was so violent that the men near the bow were thrown overboard." The bow was damaged but not pierced. The boiler was displaced, the steam pipe injured, and the wheel-house torn away. The damage was repaired in about two days.

Ives did not attempt to continue upriver with the stern-wheeler. Instead, on March 9th, he and two companions took a skiff up the Colorado and reached the mouth of Las Vegas Wash in two days. The trio then returned to the steamer.

"CHIMNEY PEAK," by H. B. Mollhousen,
depicts the design and crew of the steamer *Explorer* which was used
by the Ives expedition to reconnaissance the lower Colorado River
and to attempt to determine its head of steamer navigation.

Appearing in Ives'
Report Upon the Colorado River of the West,
"BIG CANON," from a sketch by F. W. Egloffstein,
with its companion illustrations,
made up the first pictorial account
of the Grand Canyon.

Ives decided, incorrectly, that the mouth of Black Canyon was the head of steamer navigation. The head was later set at Callville, Nevada which was located approximately thirty-five miles above the mouth of Black Canyon, an area now submerged beneath Lake Mead. Callville was planned by the Mormons as a river port to facilitate transportation of supplies between California and Utah via a water route. However, Callville was little used as a port and abandoned when the transcontinental railroad was completed in 1869. Steam navigation on the lower Colorado continued into the early years of the 20th Century by which time more than twenty-five steamboats had eventually operated on the river and formed an interesting and important period in the history of the great river.

On March 13, the Ives expedition left the mouth of Black Canyon and started a downriver voyage to meet a mule train traveling north from Yuma bringing supplies and men that would be part of the overland expedition to the Grand Canyon. Ten days later, Lieutenant Ives began his journey to the Grand Canyon with forty-four men and 150 mules.

Ives traveled into northern Arizona, approaching the Grand Canyon from the southwest. He recorded that "The famous 'Big Canon' was before us; and for a long time we paused in wondering delight, surveying that stupendous formation through which the Colorado and its tributaries break their way." They descended into the Grand Canyon via two tributaries, Peach Springs to its junction with Diamond Creek, then down the latter. According to Ives, the scenery "grew wilder and grander. The sides of the tortuous canon loftier, and before long we were hemmed in by walls two thousand feet high." He wrote that "the corresponding depth and gloom of the gaping chasms into which we were plunging, imparted an unearthly character to a way that might have resembled the portals of the infernal regions. Harsh screams issuing from aerial recesses in the canon sides and apparitions of goblin-like figures perched in the rifts and hollows of the impending cliffs, gave an odd reality to this impression."

On the night of April 2, 1858, members of the expedition camped along Diamond Creek about one mile above its junction with the Colorado. Although the Prussian artist, Mollhausen, and a few members of the party did hike to the river that evening, it was not until the morning of April 3d that Ives and the rest of the expedition reached the banks of the great river which flowed through the bottom of the Grand Canyon. Ives described the magnificent canyon as "unrivalled in grandeur."

Later, however, Ives made a most inaccurate observation when he summed his impressions of the Grand Canyon country with the statement that "the region is, of course, altogether valueless. It can be approached only from the south, and after entering it there is nothing to do but leave. Ours has been the first, and will doubtless be the last, party of whites to visit this profitless locality. It seems intended by nature that the Colorado river, along the greater portion of its lonely and majestic way, shall be forever unvisited and undisturbed."

At the mouth of Diamond Creek, Dr. Newberry, the expedition's geologist, made the first geological examination of the Grand Canyon. Ives recorded that "Dr. Newberry has had opportunities for observation seldom afforded to the geologist." Newberry measured a 3200-foot section of rock and identified many fossils. Egloffstein made a sketch of the canyon at the mouth of Diamond Creek which greatly exaggerated the walls and gave the canyon a dark and mysterious image. His sketches, with those of Mollhausen, were the first of the Grand Canyon.

The expedition left the bottom of the canyon and ascended to the surface of the surrounding country where Ives continued his exploration of the region. Accompanied by some of his men, Ives located the rim of Havasu Canyon and Mr. Egloffstein found an ancient wooden ladder which descended into the canyon. Perhaps, this was the same ladder Garces had used nearly eighty-two years earlier on his visit to the canyon and the Havasupai.

Egloffstein decided to make a descent via the ladder; however, when it received his weight, it began to collapse.

Luckily, according to Ives "one side fortunately stood firm, and holding on to this with a tight grip, he (Egloffstein) made a precipitate descent. The other side and all the rounds broke loose and accompanied him to the bottom in a general crash." Undaunted by this accident, Egloffstein continued into Havasu Canyon to witness the Indians' homes and their corn fields. Egloffstein may have been the first white man to reach the Indian village since Fray Garces in June and July of 1776. He was helped out of the canyon with a line dropped by his comrades who had remained on the rim awaiting his return.

After additional exploration of the area, the expedition journeyed to Fort Defiance. Ives then returned to Yuma and disposed of the *Explorer*. He later prepared an account of his expedition entitled, *Report Upon the Colorado River of the West*, which was published by the Government Printing Office in 1861.

How the Canyon Received Its Name.

In his report, Ives referred to the Grand Canyon as the "Big Canon." Several names have been applied to the canyon. When, in 1540, Cardenas and his expedition became the first white men to see the canyon, they apparently did not give it a name. But, in 1776, when Fray Garces saw the canyon he called it Puerto de Bucareli, "Bucareli Pass," because he saw the canyon as a river pass and chose to honor the Viceroy of New Spain, Antonio Araia Bucareli y Ursua.

By the 1850's and 1860's, the names "Big Canon" (the spelling without the letter y is the Spanish form) and "Grand Canon of the Colorado" were in use. Ives used "Big Canon" and Colonel Randolph Barnes Marcy, in an 1866 account of his army experiences in the West, used the variant "Big Canon of the Colorado." General William Jackson Palmer reported "Grand Canon of the Colorado" was in general use in Arizona by 1867. Palmer also used that name on a map published in 1869.

The names "Grand Canon" and its English equivalent, "Grand Canyon", and "Grand Canon of the Colorado" were in use by 1869 when Major John Wesley Powell made his famous exploratory voyage through the canyon. Frederick Samuel Dellenbaugh, an historian of the Colorado River and a member of Powell's second river expedition, claimed Powell gave the canyon its name. Obviously, his assertion was wrong. The English spelled form, "Grand Canyon", has become standard and is employed in governmental publications and maps.

Jacob Hamblin, the "Buckskin Apostle."

During the period from 1858 through 1864, Jacob Hamblin, a Mormon missionary, led several expeditions from southern Utah to the Grand Canyon area in attempts to reach the Hopi and Navajo Indians of northeastern Arizona. Hamblin's purposes on these treks, other than the obvious religious reasons, were to learn the Hopi language and to dissuade the Navajo from continuing their raids on Mormon settlements located in southern Utah.

These expeditions took various routes and made crossings of the Colorado River at the present site of Lee's Ferry, "The Crossing of the Fathers," and at the site of present day Pearce Ferry, two miles below the Grand Canyon. Their crossing at the Lee's Ferry site was the first recorded crossing of the Colorado River at that location.

Sitgreaves
1851

Ives
1857-58
oooooo Schooner MONTEREY
——— Steamboat EXPLORER
.... Land Route

Hamblin
—·— 1858
——+— 1859
—·—·— 1862
— — — 1863

Powell 1869
o——o River Route

Green River
Salt Lake City
GREEN RIVER
RIVER
St. George
Las Vegas
Callville
Grand Canyon
Oraibi
Ft. Defiance
Santa Fe
Zuni
COLORADO
San Diego
Phoenix
GILA R.
Yuma
Tucson

NORTON ALLEN

Splashing blue-green waters of Havasu Creek and towering walls of Havasu Canyon in the bottom of the Grand Canyon.

In the midst of a summer storm,
rays of sunlight penetrate somber skies
to light Brahma and Zoroaster Temples
near Bright Angel Point
on the North Rim.

First Boat Travel in the Canyon.

The first known boat travel in the Grand Canyon occurred in 1864. A prospecting party consisting of Octavius Decatur Gass, James Ferry, a man named Butterfield and an Indian embarked from El Dorado Canyon, downriver from the Grand Canyon, and boated up the Colorado. They entered the canyon at its western portal, the Grand Wash Cliffs, and pulled their boat nineteen miles upriver. The quartet's inexperience with rapids caused a halt to the river venture. Before returning downriver, the men erected two rock monuments, one on each bank, to mark the point they had reached.

Early Downriver Expeditions.

Several Green or Colorado River descents apparently were ended or aborted short of reaching the upper end of the Grand Canyon.

In the Spring of 1825, General William Henry Ashley accompanied by a party of trappers descended a stretch of the upper Green River to near the head of Desolation Canyon in Utah. Their voyage was made in bull-boats. The frames for these craft were constructed of long poles (approximately 30 feet) which were covered by buffalo hides. Ashley's river expedition terminated over 400 miles upstream from the Grand Canyon.

In 1831, fur trappers Luis Ambrois and Jose Jessum are reported to have trapped and boated down the Green to the Colorado, then down the Colorado where rapids forced them to abandon their voyage. Ambrois and Jessum probably met defeat in the rough water of Cataract Canyon which begins two hundred miles upriver from the Grand Canyon.

Trapper Denis Julien carved two 1836 inscriptions along the lower Green and another near the end of Cataract Canyon. These historic graffiti suggest that Julien may have boated stretches of the Green and Colorado. His Cataract Canyon mark is over 185 miles from the Grand Canyon.

In 1849, William Lewis Manly and six comrades, intent on reaching California, took a dilapidated ferry and started down the Green. When the ferry hung on a rock; the trip continued in canoes to below the Book Cliffs, near the site of present-day Green River, Utah, where they abandoned the canoes in favor of an overland route.

In 1860, prospector John D. Henderson reported encountering three men boating on the Grand River, a tributary of the Colorado River below its confluence with the Blue River. The trio told Henderson they had started from Breckenridge, Colorado and were bound for California.

Lieutenant Randolph Marcy, in 1866, reported: "The mountaineers in Utah told me that a party of trappers many years since built a large row-boat and made the attempt to descend the river through the defile of the canon, but were never heard from afterward." Marcy conjectured "They probably dashed their boat in pieces, and were lost by being precipitated over sunken rocks or elevated falls." This purported trip probably did not reach the Grand Canyon and no other record of the mysterious boaters and their voyage has been found.

In 1867, three Mormons, including the aforementioned Jacob Hamblin, employed a sixteen-foot skiff to explore the Colorado River from the lower end of the Grand Canyon to Callville, Nevada. The trio passed the mouth of the Virgin River, passed through Boulder Canyon and landed at Callville, boating a distance of about sixty-five miles.

Samuel Adams, who used the title of Captain, declared that he had explored the Colorado River during the years 1864 through 1867. In 1870, Adams unsuccessfully petitioned Congress for $20,000 to cover his asserted work.

Fragmentary reports exist of other early downriver boating ventures. Unfortunately, records of early navigation of the Green and Colorado Rivers are incomplete. Undoubtedly, some early boating attempts occurred for which there are no reports.

James White, Was He the First?

Three persons have laid claim to the title and honor of being the first through the Grand Canyon by water.

John Moss stated that, in 1861, he made a four-day raft trip through the canyon, but no serious credence has been given this alleged boating activity.

Another claimant, though, has spurred much debate about the authenticity of his voyage and there are those who believe his story. On September 7, 1867, an exhausted James White, aboard a log raft, floated to the river bank at Callville. White, suffering from severe exposure, recounted an exciting story.

He claimed to have been on a prospecting trip with Captain Charles Baker and George Strole. According to White, Baker was killed in a fight with Indians, but White and Strole escaped to the Colorado River where they built a log raft and set off downstream. On the fourth day, Strole drowned in a large rapid.

White claimed the river journey lasted sixteen days and that he traveled the entire length of the Grand Canyon. Indeed, if the voyage was as White had related, his would have been an historic first.

White's account of prospecting with Baker and Strole is generally accepted, but his story of rafting completely through the Grand Canyon is highly doubtful. During late summer, the season White was on the Colorado, the flow of the river was low and travel would have been impeded by pools of still water, sand bars, and rapids with insufficient water for navigation. A trip under such conditions would necessitate lining and portaging of rapids, strenuous rowing and would require at least twenty-five days. Yet, White maintained that he covered almost the entire distance by himself on a crude raft, with practically no food, in just over two weeks.

A not too shapely,
yet ruggedly handsome yucca
puts forth its creamy bloom
in one of the virtually inaccessible,
unnamed side canyons of the grand abyss.

From Mile 120.

Pages 34 and 35.
The great Redwall Cavern
and the Marble Gorge.

White's description of the canyon through which he floated does not fit the Grand Canyon and in subsequent retellings of his story, White changed his account of some events and facts.

It is indisputable that White traveled along the Colorado on a raft for he was observed by witnesses at Callville. The debate arises over the length of river he traveled. Colorado River historian Robert Brewster Stanton, who interviewed White in 1907, felt he commenced his voyage near the Grand Wash Cliffs at the western end of the Grand Canyon and about sixty-four miles upriver from Callville. Several other points of embarkation have also been suggested and considered by students of the history of the Colorado River and White is not without supporters for being the first to voyage through the Grand Canyon.

It remains a distinct probability that James White was not the first to navigate the entire length of the Grand Canyon. This historic honor belongs to Major John Wesley Powell and his five man crew who, in 1869, made the first documented water transit of the Grand Canyon. Their story is a momentous and adventurous part of the Grand Canyon saga.

Moist canyon walls
dampened and cooled
by small springs
provide a habitat
for these fragile
shooting stars.

33

John Wesley Powell
and the "Exploration of the Colorado River of the West."

John Wesley Powell was born at Mount Morris, New York on March 24, 1834. His parents, Joseph and Mary, were immigrants from England and, with their family of eight children, moved several times during Powell's childhood.

Because of these various family moves, John Wesley received only fragmentary early formal education. From 1852 to 1861, he divided his time between farming, teaching, attending college and pursuing independent scientific field trips. At the age of 27, Powell enlisted in the Twentieth Illinois Volunteer Infantry.

In April of 1862, Powell participated in the battle of Shiloh. During the fight, Captain Powell's right forearm was struck by a minie ball, necessitating amputation of his arm below the elbow. Later, Powell took part in the battles of Vicksburg and Nashville and on September 18, 1864 was promoted to the rank of major.

Powell requested and, on January 4, 1865, was granted a discharge from the Army due to disability. Even after his discharge Powell was referred to as the Major.

Powell conceived the idea of an expedition to the Rocky Mountains and on June 1, 1867 the expedition commenced. The party consisted of eleven men and Mrs. Powell. The result of this expedition, Powell said, "was to kindle a desire to explore the canyons of the Grand, Green and Colorado Rivers."

The following year, Powell made trips to the Grand and Yampa Rivers and made two excursions down the White River to the Green. Powell said that during these trips "I siezed every opportunity to study the canyons through which these streams run, and while thus engaged formed plans for the exploration of the canyons of the Colorado."

He studied the available maps and documents relative to the area and talked with people familiar with sections of the country through which his expedition would pass. He read the report by Lieutenant Joseph C. Ives of his 1857-58 exploration of the lower stretch of the Colorado River and the western portion of the Grand Canyon and was reported to have interviewed James White about his alleged 1867 raft trip through the canyon.

Determined to make the trip, Powell began to organize and equip his expedition. Financial assistance sought from Congress was unsuccessful, but Ulysses S. Grant, then President, was approached and authorized Powell to draw rations from Army

"Grand Canon of the Colorado. (6,200 feet deep.)"
Powell's "Exploration of the Colorado River of the West."

"We are now ready to start on our way down the Great Unknown.

"We are three quarters of a mile in the depths of the earth, and the great river shrinks into insignificance as it dashes its angry waves against the walls and cliffs that rise to the world above; the waves are but puny ripples, and we but pigmies, running up and down the sands or lost among the boulders.

"We have an unknown distance yet to run, an unknown river to explore. What falls there are, we know not; what rocks beset the channel, we know not; what walls rise over the river, we know not. Ah, well! we may conjecture many things. The men talk as cheerfully as ever; jests are bandied about freely this morning; but to me the cheer is somber and the jests are ghastly.

"With some eagerness and some anxiety and some misgiving we enter the canyon below and are carried along by the swift water through walls which rise from its very edge."
Major Powell, August 13, 1869.

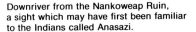
Downriver from the Nankoweap Ruin,
a sight which may have first been familiar
to the Indians called Anasazi.

posts. Contributions in the amounts of $500 were received from the Chicago Academy of Sciences, Illinois State Normal University and Illinois Industrial University. The Union Pacific and Burlington railroads gave free passage to the expedition's personnel and supplies. Scientific instruments were borrowed from the Smithsonian Institution and Illinois Industrial University. Mercurial barometers were carried to establish altitude and sextants to determine latitude and longitude.

Powell is reported to have designed the four lake-type boats, constructed in Chicago by the Bagley Boat Yard. Three of the boats were twenty-one feet long with beams of four feet and were twenty-two inches deep. These boats were named *Maid of the Canyon*, *Kitty Clyde's Sister*, and the *No Name*. The fourth boat, the *Emma Dean*, named for Powell's wife, was somewhat shorter at sixteen feet. Planked in pine, it was lighter than the other boats and was to serve as the pilot boat.

The boats were propelled by two pairs of oars and steering was by a sweep from the stern. Unfortunately, too heavy and difficult to maneuver, the boats proved to be ill-suited for fast water navigation.

Powell's crew, numbering nine men, received food and supplies, but no pay. Some of the crew had been on his 1867 and 1868 Rocky Mountain expeditions and seven had served in the Union Army during the Civil War. Major Powell and several of the men had boating knowledge, but none were skilled or had experience in rough water navigation.

Powell selected Green River, Wyoming as the embarkation point for the expedition. The Green River, the principal tributary to the Colorado, rises in the Wind River Mountains of western Wyoming. The Green flows southward into Utah, winds east into Colorado for a short distance, through Dinosaur National Monument and back into Utah. About seven hundred miles from its source, the Green reaches its confluence with the Colorado in southeastern Utah's spectacular Canyonlands National Park, 217 miles from its entrance into the Grand Canyon.

The ten man, four boat canyon expedition embarked from Green River on May 24, 1869. Powell, J. C. Sumner and William H. Dunn led the way in the small pilot boat, the *Emma Dean*. Behind were Walter Powell and George Bradley in the *Kitty Clyde's Sister*, the *No Name* manned by O. G. Howland, his brother Seneca and Frank Goodman. Last in line was the *Maid of the Canyon* carrying Billy Hawkins and Andy Hall.

"We take with us rations deemed sufficient to last ten months, for we expect, when winter comes on and the river is filled with ice, to lie over at some point until spring arrives; and so we take with us abundant supplies of clothing, likewise. We have also a large quantity of ammunition and two or three dozen traps. For the purpose of building cabins, repairing boats, and meeting other exigencies, we are supplied with axes, hammers, saws, augers, and other tools, and a quantity of nails and screws. For scientific work, we have two sextants, four chronometers, a number of barometers, thermometers, compasses, and other instruments.

"The flour is divided into three equal parts; the meat, and all other articles of our rations, in the same way. Each of the larger boats has an axe, hammer, saw, auger, and other tools, so that all are loaded alike. We distribute the cargoes in this way that we may not be entirely destitute of some important article should any one of the boats be lost. In the small boat we pack a part of the scientific instruments, three guns, and three small bundles of clothing, only; and in this I proceed in advance to explore the channel."

The voyage down the Green was not without incident. Boats had to be portaged and lined at some rapids. The *No Name* was lost in an accident at Disaster Falls in the Canyon of Lodore on June 9. The barometers were recovered from the wreckage, but one third of the expedition's rations were lost as were all of Frank Goodman's possessions. Goodman quit the party when the expedition reached the mouth of the Uinta River.

The Confluence of the Green and Colorado Rivers was reached on July 17. The expedition passed through the rough water of Cataract Canyon and down Glen Canyon and on August 4, stopped at the mouth of the little Paria River, the future site of Lee's Ferry. Powell's party was at the head of the Grand Canyon.

The Powell expedition left Lee's Ferry on August 5 and entered the 277.1 miles of the magnificent, but formidable Grand Canyon. The one-armed navigator expressed the emotions of the party when he wrote "With some feeling of anxiety we enter a new canyon this morning. We have learned to observe closely the texture of the rock. In softer strata we have quiet river, in harder we find rapids and falls. Below us are limestones and hard sandstones which we found in Cataract Canyon. This bodes toil and danger."

Powell's assessment was correct. Their transit through the canyon was difficult. They were plagued by rapids for which their boats were ill-suited. Consequently, many rapids had to be portaged or lined. A shortage of food severely sapped their energy and affected their mental outlook.

Powell incorrectly concluded the canyon's prominent Redwall Limestone was marble and named the upper sixty-one miles of the canyon, between the mouth of the little Paria River and the mouth of the Little Colorado River, Marble Canyon. The preferred name is Marble Gorge, although the incorrectness of marble remains.

Thirty-two miles from the canyon entrance, according to Powell, "The river turns sharply to the east and seems inclosed by a wall set with a million brilliant gems. What can it mean? Every eye is engaged, every one wonders. On coming nearer we find fountains bursting from the rock high overhead, and the spray in the sunshine forms the gems which bedeck the wall. The rocks below the fountain are covered with mosses and ferns and many beautiful flowering plants." Powell named the place "Vasey's Paradise" for George W. Vasey, a botanist, who was on the Major's 1868 Rocky Mountain expedition. Powell had hoped Vasey could join the river expedition, but he was unable to do so.

The Little Colorado River was reached at two o'clock on August 10. The party camped there two days, then resumed their downriver course. Powell described their apprehension when he wrote, "We are now ready to start on our way down the Great Unknown. We have but a month's rations remaining. We have an unknown distance yet to run, an unknown river to explore. With some eagerness and some anxiety and some misgiving we enter the canyon below and are carried along the swift water."

Powell stated that on August 15, "Early in the afternoon we discover a stream entering from the north—a clear, beautiful creek, coming down through a gorgeous red canyon. We land and camp on a sand beach above its mouth, under a great, overspreading tree with willow-shaped leaves." The Major first called this stream Silver Creek, but later changed its name to Bright Angel Creek.

In the western portion of the canyon, the struggling crew portaged Lava Falls, considered the river's most severe rapid. On August 27, just thirty-eight miles from the canyon's end, the exhausted party reached yet another hazardous rapid. The rapid was examined from the right bank, then from the left bank and again from the right bank before Powell decided that the rapid could be run. He informed the crew of his decision to make the run the following morning.

Then, according to Powell, "After supper Captain Howland asks to have a talk with me. We walk up the little creek a short distance, and I soon find that his object is to remonstrate against my determination to proceed. He thinks that we had better abandon the river here. Talking with him, I learn that he, his brother, and William Dunn have determined to go no farther in the boats. So we return to camp. Nothing is said to the other men.

"For the last two days our course has not been plotted. I sit down and do this now, for the purpose of finding where we are by dead reckoning. It is a clear night, and I take out the sextant to make observation for latitude, and I find that the astronomic determination agrees very nearly with that of the plot—quite as closely as might be expected from a meridian observation on a planet. In a direct line, we must be about 45 miles from the mouth of the Rio Virgen. If we can reach that point, we know that there are settlements up that river about 20 miles. This 45 miles in a direct line will probably be 80 or 90 by the meandering line of the river. But then we know that there is comparatively open country for many miles above the mouth of the Virgen, which is our point of destination.

"As soon as I determine all this, I spread my plot on the sand and wake Howland, who is sleeping down by the river, and show him where I suppose we are, and where several Mormon settlements are situated.

The "Black Depths,"
was a term applied by Major John Wesley Powell
to the granite gorges of the Grand Canyon,
where the river snatched away
the little food left to the boating party
and where the toil of passage
and a concern for survival
steadily weakened both mind and body
for the task at hand.

"We have another short talk about the morrow, and he lies down again; but for me there is no sleep. All night long I pace up and down a little path, on a few yards of sand beach, along by the river. Is it wise to go on? I go to the boats again to look at our rations. I feel satisfied that we can get over the danger immediately before us; what there may be below I know not. From our outlook yesterday on the cliffs, the canyon seemed to make another great bend to the south, and this, from our experience heretofore, means more and higher granite walls. I am not sure that we can climb out of the canyon here, and, if at the top of the wall, I know enough of the country to be certain that it is a desert of rock and sand between this and the nearest Mormon town, which, on the most direct line, must be 75 miles away. True, the late rains have been favorable to us, should we go out, for the probabilities are that we shall find water still standing in holes; and at one time I almost conclude to leave the river. But for years I have been contemplating this trip. To leave the exploration unfinished, to say that there is a part of the canyon which I cannot explore, having already nearly accomplished it, is more than I am willing to acknowledge, and I determine to go on.

"I wake my brother and tell him of Howland's determination, and he promises to stay with me; then I call up Hawkins, the cook, and he makes a like promise; then Sumner and Bradley and Hall, and they all agree to go on.

"At last daylight comes and we have breakfast without a word being said about the future. The meal is as solemn as a funeral. After breakfast I ask the three men if they still think it best to leave us. The elder Howland thinks it is, and Dunn agrees with him. The younger Howland tries to persuade them to go on with the party; failing in which, he decides to go with his brother."

Powell gave two rifles and a shotgun to the three men leaving the river. He also asked them to take their share of the remaining rations, but they declined. Hawkins, the cook, put a pan of biscuits on a rock for them.

The Howlands and Dunn did not leave at once, but remained and assisted the six voyagers in transporting two of the three boats around the first part of the rapid. The loss of the three men did not leave the expedition with adequate personnel to run all the boats, so Powell decided to abandon the *Emma Dean,* the boat which was the most severely damaged.

Powell wrote a letter to his wife which he gave to O. G. Howland. Sumner gave Howland his watch and asked that it be sent on to his sister should he not survive the voyage. Howland also took with him a duplicate set of the expedition's records.

When the two parties were ready to separate, the minority again attempted to persuade the majority to quit the river and join them in the climb from the canyon. Powell wrote. "Some tears are shed; it is rather a solemn parting; each party thinks the other is taking the dangerous course."

The Major, aboard the *Maid of the Canyon,* ran the rapid and the *Kitty Clyde's Sister* also safely negotiated the rough water which had caused the separation of the expedition's men. According to Powell, "we have passed many places that were worse."

They fired their guns to signal the Howlands and Dunn that the rapid had been successfully passed, hoping that the three men would reconsider, take the *Emma Dean* and rejoin the expedition. When, after a short wait, the trio did not appear, Powell and his men resumed their voyage.

Six and one-half miles downriver at Spencer Creek Rapid; Major Powell, Hawkins and Hall capsized and had to be rescued by Bradley who had made a successful run.

At noon on August 29, the expedition passed beneath the Grand Wash Cliffs which marked the end of the 277.4 mile voyage through the Grand Canyon. Powell described their feelings after completing the river passage, "The relief from danger and the joy of success are great ... Ever before us has been an unknown danger, heavier than immediate peril. Every waking hour passed in the Grand Canyon has been one of toil. We have watched with deep solicitude the steady disappearance of our scant supply of rations, and from time to time have seen the river snatch a portion of the little left, while we were a-hungered. And danger and toil were endured in those gloomy depths, where oftimes clouds hid the sky by day and but a narrow zone of stars could be seen at night. Only during the few hours of deep sleep, consequent on hard labor, has the roar of the waters been hushed. Now the danger is over, now the toil has ceased, now the gloom has disappeared, now the firmament is bounded only by the horizon, and what a vast expanse of constellations can be seen!

"The river rolls by us in silent majesty; the quiet of the camp is sweet; our joy is almost ecstasy. We sit till long after midnight talking of the Grand Canyon, talking of home, but talking chiefly of the three men who left us. Are they wandering in those depths, unable to find a way out? Are they searching over the desert lands above for water? Or are they nearing the settlements?" These speculations did not anticipate the true fate of their three comrades.

On August 30, 1869, the Powell expedition arrived at the mouth of the Virgin River where the 1048 mile voyage was terminated. They had been on the river 98 days, 24 of which had been spent in the Grand Canyon. John Wesley Powell and his remaining crew of five men had achieved the singular honor of being the first to pass through the Grand Canyon by water.

The Major and his brother, Walter Powell, left at the Virgin River and journeyed to Salt Lake City; but the other four crew members continued on downriver. Bradley and Sumner boated another 353 miles to Yuma, Arizona, 1401 miles from Green River, Wyoming and Hall and Hawkins took their boat to tidewater at the head of the Gulf of California. Their journey had covered 1517 miles, the first to boat from Wyoming to the Gulf of California.

The fate of the Howland brothers and William Dunn is subject to conjecture as reports of events subsequent to their leaving the Powell expedition are incomplete and not always in agreement.

"Climbing in the Grand Canyon."
From Powell's "Exploration of the Colorado River of the West."

After watching Powell and his men plunge their two boats into the rapid they had declined to run, the three men apparently followed a northeast trending tributary canyon, away from the river's north bank. Upon reaching the canyon rim, it is likely that they traveled north toward the Mormon settlements in southern Utah.

Several days later, an Indian reported that three white men had recently been killed by Shevwits Indians. A telegram with this same news was received at St. George, Utah on September 7, 1869. On his trip to Salt Lake City, Powell had made unsuccessful inquiries as to the whereabouts of the three and learned of their tragic deaths upon his arrival in the Utah capital on September 15.

Several reports seemed to bear out the authenticity of the story that the men had been slain by the Shevwits. A party of Shevwits was reported to have appeared in St. George attempting to trade several items which evidently had belonged to white men. The Indians said they had found the articles at an abandoned camp. One of the Shevwits, To-ab, had a watch. O. G. Howland had carried a watch given to him by Jack Sumner for safekeeping.

Wanting to learn more about the deaths of the Howlands and Dunn, Major Powell accompanied Mormon President Brigham Young to Kanab, Utah in September, 1870. He also wanted the assurance of the Shevwits that they would not act hostilely toward an expedition he planned for the year 1871. Upon President Young's recommendation, Powell contacted Jacob Hamblin for assistance and the "Buckskin Apostle" agreed to organize an expedition to reach the Shevwits. Upon contacting the Indians, Hamblin explained the purpose of their visit, noting that reports laid the blame for the killings on the Shevwits. The Indians readily admitted the slayings, claiming that they were justified since they had been told by Indians living across the Colorado that prospectors there had abused Indian women and that if prospectors found precious metals in the country of the Shevwits, the Indians would be driven from their homes. Powell's men were charged with being prospectors who should be killed before they discovered any precious metals.

In 1923, an elderly Shevwits named Old Simon gave additional credence to the reports. He recalled that, in his youth, three white men had climbed from the Grand Canyon and encountered a group of his people. Although most of the Indians were in favor of letting the whites live; one Indian, To-ab, especially wanted to kill them and refused to accept the majority opinion. He persuaded two of his comrades to accompany him and they, according to Old Simon, committed the murders in an ambush.

There were also stories that the Howlands and Dunn had come upon an Indian squaw gathering seed, shot her, and were killed by the Shevwits in retaliation. Other reports suggested that the men were not killed by Indians, but by other white men since "The Indians got a lot of blame for some things they didn't do."

The rapid that caused the unfortunate three men to abandon the river was originally named "Catastrophe Rapid", but is now known as Separation Rapid. The side canyon they followed to their mysterious deaths is now also named Separation. These names do not indicate that the three men deserted Major Powell, as is sometimes stated, but left with the

47

Steep to nearly vertical limestone walls of the Marble Gorge
rise abruptly from the banks of the Colorado River
and characterize the Grand Canyon's first 61 miles
of wilderness rock corridor.

Major's consent and, according to Powell, were given records of the expedition. Fellow crewman George Bradley said, "They left us with good feelings though we deeply regret their loss for they are as fine fellows as I ever had the good fortune to meet."

Two plaques which were placed near Separation Rapid commemorate the three slain men.

In 1871, Major Powell undertook a second river expedition for a more extensive investigation of the river canyons and surrounding country. This expedition received $10,000 in financial assistance from Congress and was provided with better equipment and support than the earlier voyage.

Although benefiting from knowledge gained on the 1869 expedition, Powell did not attempt to acquire boats of a better design. The Major maintained the boats "were well adapted for the purpose." Although slightly longer with a mid-compartment for storage, the three new boats were of the basic type used in 1869. They were named the *Emma Dean,* the *Nellie Powell,* and the *Canonita.* A chair was secured to the top of the *Emma Dean's* mid-compartment enabling Powell to be "comfortable and see well ahead."

The party numbered eleven, none of whom had been on the 1869 trip and none were skilled boatmen. A photographer and a cartographer were included in the crew.

Powell's second voyage began on May 22, 1871 at Green River, Wyoming and reached Lee's Ferry on October 22, 1871. There the expedition was discontinued for nearly ten months, supplies and equipment being cached for the resumption of the voyage. Much of the cache of material was stolen by a group of ten prospectors who set off down-river on rafts. About eleven miles below Lee's Ferry, in Soap Creek Rapid, the rafts were destroyed and the supplies lost.

The second half of Major Powell's second river expedition began on August 17, 1872 with two boats, the *Emma Dean,* and the *Canonita* and a party numbering seven men.

At Kanab Creek, about 51 percent of the way through the Grand Canyon, the voyage was terminated falling considerably short of a water transit through the canyon.

A pack train met the expedition at Kanab Creek ending Major Powell's historic boating career in the Grand Canyon.

Powell prepared a report about his exploration of the Colorado River which was published by the government in 1875. In the publication, Powell detailed the 1869 expedition.

In 1879, Major Powell was appointed to a commission to codify the public land laws. He became the second director of the U. S. Geological Survey in 1881 and served in that capacity until 1894. Powell was instrumental in the establishment of the Geological Society of America and was an organizer of the National Geographic Society. He was also the head of the Bureau of Ethnology, a position he held until his death in 1902.

The Powell Memorial, located on Sentinel Point at the South Rim of the Grand Canyon was dedicated on May 20, 1918 to commemorate the Major and the five men of his crew who completed the 1869 expedition.

The Wheeler Upriver Expedition.

In the same year that Powell began his second canyon voyage, Army Lieutenant George Montague Wheeler led an expedition up the Colorado River and into the western Grand Canyon. The Wheeler expedition embarked at Camp Mohave and traveled about 141 miles upriver to the foot of the canyon and then 52 miles further to Diamond Creek. The party numbered thirty-four men, including fourteen Mohave Indians who provided the man power to pull the three flat bottomed, square sterned skiffs and, for part of the distance, a supply barge. The fifty-two miles to Diamond Creek was the deepest upriver penetration of the canyon until the 1940's when Harry Leroy Aleson began his attempts to take a power boat up the canyon.

Hance Rapid, Mile 76.7, was named for John Hance; a prospector, miner, guide and colorful canyon character. A canyon visitor once wrote,
"Captain John Hance—a genius, a philosopher, and a poet, the possessor of a fund of information vastly important, if true. He laughs with the giddy, yarns to the gullible, talks sense to the sedate, and is a most excellent judge of scenery, human nature and pie. To see the canyon only, and not to see Captain John Hance, is to miss half the show."

From Yaki Point.

Prospectors, Miners and Artists; Colorful Characters of Early Canyon Settlement.

Prospecting and mining led to much of the early exploration and development of the Grand Canyon. Who the first prospectors were and when they entered the canyon is unknown, but one of the earliest prospectors was William H. Hardy who searched for precious metals in Havasu Canyon in 1866.

George Riley, one of three men to explore Kanab Canyon with Major John Wesley Powell in 1871, found gold at the mouth of Kanab Creek. Reports of his find caused a minor gold rush. Gold was found, but in such quantities that the economic return did not justify the work. The rush lasted about four months and was over by June of 1872 although a few prospectors continued to search the canyon for precious metals.

In June, 1873, Charles Spencer found silver in Havasu Canyon, a few hundred yards below beautiful Havasu Falls.

William Ridenour and his partner, S. Crozier, prospected in the canyon in 1874, but were driven out by hostile Indians.

In 1879, a five man prospecting party, reportedly led by W. C. Beckman and H. J. Young, discovered carbonate of lead in Havasu Canyon and lead, silver and vanadium were later mined in the canyon. Platinum was reportedly located in Havasu Canyon.

Prospecting and mining activity along both the North and South rims increased in the 1880's and 1890's. In 1880, Seth B. Tanner helped organize the Little Colorado Mining District. He located a small silver and copper mine near the mouth of Palisades Creek, about four miles below the Little Colorado River and in 1889, Tanner, with the aid of two friends, improved an old Indian trail leading into the canyon to gain better access to the mine. The original trail left the canyon rim west of Cedar Mountain. The present Tanner Trail heads near Lipan Point and reaches the Colorado River at Tanner Canyon Rapid.

The northern Arizona town of Flagstaff was settled in 1876. In 1882, Edward Everett Ayer established the first lumber mill, an industry that became important to the economy of the town. The transcontinental railroad reached Flagstaff in the same year and interest began to develop in the scenic features of the area, particularly the magnificent Grand Canyon.

50

The United States Geological Survey conducted a study of the canyon in 1880 and 1881. The expedition was led by Clarence Edward Dutton who named many canyon landforms for deities, many of which were tied to ancient civilizations. Dutton wrote the first geological monograph on the Grand Canyon which contained illustrations prepared by artists William Henry Holmes and Thomas Moran.

Artists did much to acquaint the American public with the singular beauty of the Grand Canyon. Prominent among the early canyon artists was English-born Thomas Moran, one of the great landscape painters of the 19th century, who worked at the Grand Canyon for twelve winters as well as other lengthy periods.

In the early 1880's, John Hance, who was to become a famous canyon character, claimed land at the South Rim and was the first white resident of the canyon. Hance built the South Rim's first tourist facility, a log cabin, located east of the present Canyon Village and advertised guided tours into the canyon.

Hance also prospected and located an asbestos mine on the north side of the canyon. In order to reach the mine, he developed an old Indian trail which led from the South Rim, near his tourist accommodations, through Red Canyon to the river, a trail he also used to conduct his tourist hikes into the canyon.

The first Grand Canyon hotel was constructed in 1884, not at the location of contemporary tourist facilities, but to the west, near the mouth of Diamond Creek at the bottom of the canyon. A twenty-two mile stage road brought tourists from the railroad at Peach Springs. The hotel closed in 1889.

John Hance operated his tourist facilities until 1895, then spent the remainder of his life as a trail guide and story-teller at Grand Canyon Village. When he was once asked how things were at the Grand Canyon, Hance replied that the tourists were throwing so many rocks into the chasm that it was in danger of filling up. Upon being informed by a tourist that trees breathed through their leaves, Hance responded that he already knew that because he had once camped under a mesquite tree that kept him awake all night with its snoring. He also said that the Colorado River was so thick with mud and silt that when he took a drink from it, he had to use his pocket knife to cut off the water.

Probably the best known story told by Hance was about the time the canyon was so full of clouds that he put on snowshoes and started to walk across to the opposite rim. When he was part way across, the clouds suddenly began to dissipate and he just made it.

The colorful Grand Canyon pioneer settler was greatly appreciated by canyon locals and tourists alike. William "Buckey" O'Neill, a canyon prospector and Yavapai County sheriff, said "God made the canyon, John Hance the trails. Without the other, neither would be complete."

A canyon visitor once wrote, "Captain John Hance — a genius, a philosopher, and a poet, the possessor of a fund of information vastly important, if true. He laughs with the giddy, yarns to the gullible, talks sense to the sedate, and is a most excellent judge of scenery, human nature and pie. To see the canyon only, and not to see Captain John Hance, is to miss half the show."

John Hance, the Grand Canyon's first white settler and unique character, died in 1919 and was buried at the cemetery at Grand Canyon Village.

William Wallace Bass arrived in Williams, Arizona in 1883 and, in 1890, moved to the canyon, establishing a camp west of Havasupai Point, some twenty-five miles west of Grand Canyon Village. Bass began prospecting, located asbestos and copper, and developed an asbestos mine on the north side of the Colorado River. In 1908, he installed a cable crossing near Mile 108.

Bass operated tourist facilities and a guide service at his camp and was a promoter of tourism, making several trips to the eastern states to develop tourist traffic.

In 1892, he met Ada Diefendorf, a tourist from New York. Two years later they were married and subsequently raised the first white family at the canyon.

"Running a Rapid,"
From Powell's "Exploration of the Colorado River of the West."

Bass operated his tourist camp and guide service until 1923. In 1925, he sold his property to the Santa Fe Land and Improvement Company, associated with the Fred Harvey Company, operator of other Grand Canyon tourist accommodations and services.

William Wallace Bass died in 1933 at the age of 84. In compliance with his request; he was cremated and his ashes, which had been placed in a copper box, were taken by airplane and dropped on a butte in the canyon. The butte is called Bass Tomb, but is also known as Holy Grail Temple.

There were many others who prospected in the Grand Canyon, three of whom were prominent; Peter D. Berry, Daniel L. Hogan, and Louis D. Boucher.

Berry, along with the Cameron brothers, Ralph and Niles, was instrumental in building the Bright Angel Trail to Indian Gardens. It was originally an Indian trail on which improvements were made.

Berry located the "Last Chance" copper claim on Horseshoe Mesa, below Grandview Point and, in 1892 and 1893, built the Grand View Trail to the mine. He was also associated with the two-story log hotel, constructed in 1895, on Grand View Point. The building no longer stands.

Hogan found copper below Maricopa Point in 1893 and operated the Lost Orphan Mine for several years. In 1936, Hogan built the Grand Canyon Trading Post on the rim above the mine and later sold both the mine and the trading post. Under different owners, the business was known as Kachina Lodge, Rogers' Place and Grand Canyon Inn.

Louis D. Boucher, a French-Canadian, was another in the long list of prospectors who also catered to tourists. Arriving at the Grand Canyon about 1891, Boucher established himself at Dripping Spring. Because of the isolated location, he became incorrectly known as a hermit. Boucher built tourist cabins at the copper mine which bore his name and he planted an orchard, but his mining and tourist ventures did not last and he had left the canyon by 1912.

Malgosa Crest
and the Colorado River
in the Marble Gorge of the Grand Canyon.

The Disastrous Brown-Stanton River Survey.

In 1889, S.S. Harper initiated a chain of events which eventually resulted in the second boat trip to pass completely through the Grand Canyon. Harper, a prospector, saw the survey line for a transcontinental railway and conceived the notion of a low grade rail route which would follow the Colorado River instead of a winding crossing of the western mountains.

Later, in Denver, the lone prospector interested Frank Mason Brown, a successful real estate businessman, in the idea. Brown became enthusiastic about the scheme and organized the Denver, Colorado Canon, and Pacific Railroad. The projected railway would follow the Colorado River from Grand Junction to Yuma, Arizona and then turn west to the Pacific coast to the port city of San Diego.

The railroad's route was not its only unusual feature; it was to be electrically powered, the power to be generated by the river.

The prime reason offered for the construction of the railroad was to haul coal from Colorado to California. Approximately nine-tenths of the coal imported to San Diego came from Australia and British Columbia and these two areas, plus England, provided about two-thirds of the coal imported to San Francisco. The planned railroad would connect the Colorado coal fields with California and substantially lower the cost of providing coal to the cities on the Pacific coast.

It was thought that the railway would open new areas for development along its route, particularly mining regions in the canyons. In addition, it was hoped that the railroad's canyon route would prove to be a popular tourist attraction.

On March 28, 1889, only three days after the organization of the railroad company, the route's field survey began at Grand Junction, Colorado. Under the direction of Frank C. Kendrick, the assistant engineer, the first portion of the work followed the Colorado River to the mouth of the Green River in Utah. Kendrick completed his survey on May 4, 1889 and returned to Denver to report to the railroad's president, Frank Brown.

Walls of the Marble Gorge as viewed from inside Redwall Cavern.
The first 61 miles of the Grand Canyon were named the Marble Canyon
by John Wesley Powell, who mistakenly
decided that the Redwall Limestone of the gorge was marble.
Today, although the erroneous terminology of marble is still applied,
the more commonly used name is Marble Gorge.

With his chief engineer, Robert Brewster Stanton, Brown and a party of fourteen men resumed the survey at Green River. Embarking from the town of Green River, Utah on May 25, 1889, the party descended the Green to its confluence with the Colorado, making a sketchy reconnaissance for a branch line down the Green to the proposed Colorado River railroad.

They proceeded down the Colorado not without many hardships. Some of the supplies and two of the six boats were lost. Three men left the party and a new one joined. Finally, the expedition was divided into two groups, one to do a field instrument survey to Lee's Ferry and the other to conduct a general and photographic reconnaissance through the Grand Canyon.

The latter group boated to Lee's Ferry and continued downriver into the Marble Gorge. On July 10, 1889, Brown's boat capsized in a rapid twelve miles below Lee's Ferry. Brown was drowned, but his body was never found. Peter M. Hansbrough, one of the crew, carved a commemorative inscription on the rocky cliff near the spot where the drowning occurred.

The saddened expedition, now under the command of Stanton, continued its downriver voyage; but five days later Hansbrough and Henry C. Richards drowned in a rapid at Mile 25.2 when their boat capsized. Richards' body was never recovered, but Hansbrough's bones were found the next year. They were buried at the base of the left wall of Marble Gorge opposite Point Hansbrough, named in his honor.

Following the drownings, Stanton decided to temporarily abandon the survey which had reached a point roughly thirty miles below Lee's Ferry. Their equipment and supplies were cached in what is now called Stanton's Cave located in the west canyon wall 150 feet above the river and one-tenth of a mile upriver from Vasey's Paradise.

"View from camp at the mouth of the Little Colorado, looking west."
From Powell's "Exploration of the Colorado River of the West."

Stanton resumed the railroad survey on December 10, 1889 with a new party consisting of twelve men, four of whom had been on the previous trip. Three new boats, much heavier than those used on the first voyage, were employed on this survey and life preservers were also carried. Problems again plagued this expedition. Nims, the photographer, broke his leg and was evacuated from Marble Gorge. In Horn Creek Rapid, a boat was lost. One man quit the party at Crystal Creek while three more left at Diamond Creek.

In spite of their problems, Stanton and the six remaining crewmen did continue the survey and on April 26, 1890, the expedition reached tidewater at the Gulf of California.

Stanton later studied an overland route for the proposed line between the Colorado River at Yuma and San Diego, but although the Denver, Colorado Canon, and Pacific Railroad was a curious and bold idea which was possible from an engineering standpoint, the railroad was not to be. Economic conditions never came to favor the venture, although the line's field survey did result in an historic second venturesome water trip through the Grand Canyon.

A Voyage for Trapping, Pleasure and Thrills.

George F. Flavell, an able boatman and trapper, and his companion, Ramon Montos formed the third party of boaters to navigate the length of the Grand Canyon. A successful and safe venture, the voyage was for trapping, pleasure and thrills. Flavell kept a diary of his canyon excursion which he prefaced with the statement that it was written more for his "own amusement than for anything else".

On August 27, 1896, "as the whistle blew for the noon hour," the two pushed their boat into the river at Green River, Wyoming and began what Flavell anticipated would be a "very interesting, if not dangerous trip".

The waters of the Green and Colorado Rivers were navigated with little trouble and "after 7 days winding and twisting through Glen Canyon, with its sluggish waters and barren peaks," the two adventurers arrived at Lee's Ferry where they were "received by a Billy Goat, 3 pups, and 2 hogs, but nothing that could talk." Finally, they found some Indians and the ferryman. They remained four days at the ferry in preparing their boat, the *Panthon*, for the trip ahead. Embarking on the 17th of October, they entered the Marble Gorge. Flavell wrote they were going "in the regions of the unknown, and if we should by accident or mismanagement, stay, why, Farewell!"

They reached the end of the gorge on October 20 where Flavell reported, "It was nothing but bail and shiver all day" and that they "ran somewhere in the vicinity of 40 rapids" and "had at least half that many barrels of water in the boat."

The companions passed out of the canyon on October 30, 1896 and several days later arrived at Needles, California. Montos left the voyage, but Flavell continued downriver to Ehrenburg, Arizona and then on to Yuma. There he concluded his voyage of adventure aboard the *Panthon*. At the conclusion of the voyage, Flavell recorded, "The trip is ended. 1685 miles of passing scenery. Gone! I am ready for another trip . . . I guess I had better hesitate a moment at least."

Nathaniel T. Galloway, the Stern First Technique.

One of the outstanding boatmen of the Green and Colorado Rivers was Nathaniel T. Galloway, a Utah trapper and prospector. Galloway's boating experience led him to develop a lightweight boat and introduce the stern-first method of navigating rapids, innovations which were widely adopted by other boaters. Galloway became the first man to boat twice through the Grand Canyon, first in 1897 and again in 1909.

"Hum Woolley."

The fifth known water transit of the Grand Canyon occurred in 1903. This voyage did not receive publicity at the time and remained unknown to historians for many years. In 1949, Otis "Dock" Marston learned that, near the turn of the century, three prospectors had embarked on a canyon voyage from Lee's Ferry. The trip, however, remained an enigma until a chance meeting between Plez Talmadge Reilly and Arthur Randall Sanger in late 1951 at Los Angeles. Sanger, one of the prospectors, told historian Reilly about the voyage. Sanger also had his diary of the trip which gave additional details. With this information, plus research by Reilly and Marston into the voyage's background and participants, the story of the fifth canyon water transit emerged.

The voyage had its origin in Los Angeles where Mrs. Jacques Traves, a widow, lived. "Madame Schell," as she was also called, had some low grade gold claims, the "Buck" and "San Bernadino," near Quartzsite, Arizona. She wanted assessment work done and hired a friend, Elias Benjamin "Hum" Woolley to do the work.

Little is known of "Hum" Woolley's personal history. He was born on May 28, 1843, probably in North Carolina. He is reported to have spent time in southeastern Colorado at Lamar, to have been a prospector, and to have boated on the Colorado prior to 1903. He may have been involved in mining activity below the Grand Canyon or upriver from the canyon in Glen

Historically,
the Fineleaf White Ragwood
has been an herb
of multiple medicinal
purposes to the Indians
of the
Grand Canyon region.

Espejo Butte
and
Comanche Point.

Looking west from Desert View on a hazy summer afternoon,
the Grand Canyon seems to go on without end,
a vast and interminable vision of chasm and desert peaks extending into infinity.

Pages 60-61
The setting sun momentarily penetrates a storm blackened sky
illuminating peaks and deep side canyons across the great abyss
from Mather Point.

Canyon. Woolley chose a seemingly roundabout way to reach the gold claims belonging to Madame Schell. Because the claims were over 225 miles below the western terminus of the Grand Canyon, they could have been reached by a fairly direct route from Los Angeles, but Woolley set a route which included boating through the Grand Canyon. Obviously "Hum" was interested in more than just completing the assessment work. Apparently he also wanted to prospect the river course through the magnificent canyon.

For the trip, Woolley constructed a boat in the back yard of Madame Schell's Los Angeles house. The flat bottomed boat was eighteen feet long, had a beam of just over four feet, and weighed more than 300 pounds. The craft was disassembled and shipped overland to Lee's Ferry.

In Los Angeles, Woolley hired Sanger, then twenty-three years old, and John Aaron King, a thirty-one year old physician.

On September 1, 1901, after reassembling the boat, the three prospectors embarked on the voyage from Lee's Ferry with the sixty-year old Woolley at the oars. On September 4, Sanger wrote in his diary: "Thank God we are still alive, it is impossible to describe what we went through today. Only the wonderful river knowledge and oarsmanship of Hum Woolley saved us from the vortex we went through, but we camped on a sandy bar with the river as meek as a lamb murmuring beside us. We are all wet and cold. It is impossible to describe the terrifying grandness of this canyon. Only God could do this. Will pray for tomorrow."

On the twenty-first day of the voyage, the boaters passed the Grand Wash Cliffs to emerge from the depths of the canyon.

Woolley and his crew stayed at Grand Wash for several days. When they resumed the downriver course, there was a new passenger, Charles Bolster, a prospector. The four men arrived at Ehrenberg on October 10th where they left the river to proceed overland to Madame Schell's gold claims north of Quartzsite. In late October, after completion of the assessment work, they returned to their boat and planned to follow the river to the Gulf of California; however, soon after passing Yuma, the water became too shallow to proceed and the foursome abandoned the river expedition.

A Voyage of Alteration and Strange Circumstance.

Four years after Hum Woolley and his two boating companions completed their Grand Canyon voyage, another threesome of prospectors embarked for a run through the canyon.

The voyage had its origin in 1899 when Albert Loper and Charles Silver Russell met at the mining town of Telluride in the San Juan Mountains of Colorado. Bert Loper subsequently proposed a prospecting trip along the Colorado River to include the Grand Canyon stretch. Loper had gained some boating experience in August, 1894 while prospecting on the San Juan River, a tributary of the Colorado. But it was not until the autumn of 1907 that the Loper promoted river prospecting trip with Russell began. By then, Loper had also interested young Edwin Regan Monett in the venture and he joined as the third man in the party.

Three galvanized steel hulled boats were ordered from the Michigan Steel Boat Company. Each was sixteen feet long and had a beam of four feet. Loper's boat was named the *Arizona*, Russell rowed the *Utah*, and Monett the *Nevada*.

Russell had made an agreement with *The Salt Lake City Tribune* to publish articles he would write about the trip and there was hope that photographs they would take of the spectacular canyon scenery would result in monetary returns.

Leaving Green River, Utah on September 20, 1907, they passed through the quiet waters of the Green's Labyrinth and Stillwater Canyons, reached the confluence of the Green and Colorado, and on September 26th began the run through the rapids of Cataract Canyon.

In Cataract's Clearwater Rapid, on October 3rd, Loper's *Arizona* struck and hung on a rock. Although the boat was freed, it was flooded, the camera damaged and the film ruined.

The voyagers reached Hite, at the upper end of Glen Canyon, and sent the camera to Eastman Kodak Company to be repaired. They visited some of the mining operations in the area and did some prospecting.

On November 1, after disagreement with Loper over his financial contributions to the trip, Russell and Monett departed and Loper remained to await the return of the camera. Russell and Monett proceeded downriver, prospecting along the way, and planned to rendezvous with Loper at Lee's Ferry. Loper was to meet them on November 21, but not later than December 1.

Russell and Monett did arrive at Lee's Ferry on November 21st and awaited the anticipated appearance of Loper. Loper received the repaired camera on November 30th, but he did not depart for Lee's Ferry until January 1, 1908, thirty-two days after he had received the repaired camera and nineteen days after the deadline for the rendezvous. Loper reached the meeting place on January 8, only to find that Russell and Monett had waited for him until December 13, when they decided that he was not coming and, concerned about winter weather, the pair departed downriver to continue their prospecting voyage. Russell left a letter addressed to Loper which stated that he and Monett would boat to Bright Angel Trail, about 88 miles into the Grand Canyon, and there climb to the South Rim.

Leaves and bracts of a cluster of Indian paintbrush burst into crimson color on a meadow of the canyon's North Rim. Of interest is the yellow-green flower of this plant which is enclosed by the red leaves and usually goes unnoticed.

Elves Chasm,
a tiny fall of water cascading over gracefully curving travertine formations,
lies hidden in one of the many small side canyons of the Grand Canyon.
Secret places such as this are revealed only to those
who would brave a once in a lifetime water transit of the canyon.

Loper did not attempt to rejoin his partners. In later years, he established himself at Red Canyon, downriver from Hite, where he lived for a time as a semi-hermit.

After losing one boat, the *Nevada*, to a rising river; Russell and Monett did reach Bright Angel Trail on January 3, where they climbed to the rim and stayed as guests of the El Tovar. On January 6, they returned to their remaining boat, the *Utah*, and continued downriver. At Hermit Rapid, the *Utah* broke away as it was being lined and the boatless pair were forced to abandon the river. Russell and Monett encountered Louis D. Boucher, the "hermit", and were invited to stay the night at his cabin. Boucher thought the lost boat could be found circling in an eddy at the mouth of Boucher Canyon.

Russell and Monett looked for and found the *Utah* where Boucher had thought it would be and after repairs were concluded, the two continued their voyage, arriving at Needles, California on February 8, 1908 where their journey ended.

Theirs was the sixth complete Grand Canyon water transit, the first trip through the canyon in a metal boat; however, the circumstances of Loper's separation from the party has resulted in much controversy and has become of great interest to historians of the Colorado River and the Grand Canyon.

Galloway-Stone, the Seventh Water Transit.

In 1909, expert riverman Nathaniel Galloway and Ohio industrialist Julius Frederick Stone embarked on the canyon voyage they had first considered in 1897. Other members of the party were Charles Sharp, Raymond Austin Cogswell, and 17-year old novice boatman Seymour S. Dubendorff.

The voyage, which was to be a pleasure trip, began, as had so many others, at Green River, Wyoming. Embarkation was on September 12, 1909 and the trip ended at Needles, California on November 19.

The journey was the seventh complete water transit of the Grand Canyon, and was Galloway's second. The outstanding boatman and boat designer continued his river activities, but made no more Grand Canyon expeditions. Young Dubendorff's boat capsized twice during the trip, the second time at Mile 131.6, in the rapid which now bears his name.

The Brothers Kolb.

In 1901, the Santa Fe Railroad opened its spur line from the main line at Williams, Arizona to the South Rim of the Grand Canyon. The first train arrived at the canyon on September 17 and caused significant changes in the South Rim's commercial landscape. The railroad's station was at Grand Canyon Village and tourist traffic was directed to the facilities at the village causing a sharp decline in patronage received by Grand View Hotel, the old Hance Hotel and Bass Camp. Eventually, all of these facilities ceased operation.

One of the trains which arrived at the canyon in 1901 carried Ellsworth Leanderson Kolb who was to become an important figure in the annals of the Grand Canyon and navigation of the turbulent waters of the Green and Colorado Rivers. Ellsworth obtained employment at the Bright Angel Hotel and in 1902, was joined at the canyon by his brother, Emery. As enterprising partners, they opened a photographic business, making pictures of tourists who were taking the mule rides down the Bright Angel Trail.

Ralph Cameron, later to become a United States senator, had helped in the construction of this trail and had taken control because of mining claims he held in strategic places. Cameron charged a toll for the trail's use, but gave the Kolb brothers a right-of-way at the head of the trail where the brothers located a studio. In 1905 the Kolbs built a darkroom at Indian Gardens.

In the morning they would take photographs of trail riders beginning the descent into the canyon, then the brothers would race down the trail, often passing the riders, to their darkroom at Indian Gardens where they would develop the negative plates, make prints and then hurry back up the trail to the rim where they would sell the finished prints to the returning riders. The photographic activities of the brothers were not confined to trail riders and they familiarized themselves with the canyon country by hiking the trails and photographing the area's magnificent scenery.

In 1911, Ellsworth and Emery Kolb began a most important and historic river voyage from Green River, Wyoming to Needles, California. The expedition's main purpose was to photograph the Green River's beautiful canyons, spectacular Cataract Canyon and the magnificence of the Grand Canyon.

The voyage began on September 8. With the brothers was James Fagin, employed to help with camp chores and the cameras. They had two flat-bottomed skiffs of the Galloway design built of white cedar, sixteen feet long. At the bow and stern were compartments. Unloaded, each weighed 500 pounds and loaded, about 1200 pounds. Ellsworth's boat was called *Defiance* and Emery christened his *Edith* after his daughter. Neither of the men were accomplished boatmen although Emery had some rowing experience, but never in rapids such as they were to encounter.

The expedition proceeded down the Green, but Fagin, homesick and unaccustomed to rough canyon country or river running, left the party at Echo Park in present day Dinosaur National Monument. Ellsworth and Emery reached the confluence of the Green and Colorado Rivers on October 26, forty-eight days out of Green River. They struggled through the rapids of Cataract Canyon, while Glen Canyon was navigated without trouble.

The portion of the voyage from the head of Marble Gorge to the mouth of Bright Angel Creek was not without problems. In Soap Creek Rapid, the second major rapid in the Marble Gorge, Ellsworth was hurled from the *Defiance*. He managed to scramble back aboard. Ellsworth again attempted to run the rapid, this time in Emery's *Edith*, only to capsize in the effort. At Hance Rapid, the *Defiance* was portaged, but Emery decided to run the rapid in the *Edith* and was thrown overboard. Uninjured, he struggled back into his boat.

Five hours after leaving Hance Rapid, the Kolbs reached the mouth of Bright Angel Creek, after sixty-nine days on the river. They set a signal fire which was seen through a telescope by Emery's wife and daughter who were over six miles away at their home on the canyon rim.

The Kolbs took a one month hiatus in their canyon voyage during which Thomas Moran, the famous Grand Canyon artist, examined several photographs the brothers had taken on their voyage. On December 19, Ellsworth and Emery returned to their boats. Bert Lauzon was employed as an assistant and the Kolb's younger brother, Ernest, desiring to take a ride on one of the boats, accompanied the party for about twenty miles. He climbed from the canyon at the Bass Trail.

At Waltenberg Rapid, on December 24, Ellsworth capsized in the *Defiance* and Emery's *Edith* hung up on rocks, was damaged, but was freed and brought to shore. The *Edith* was repaired on Christmas Day and the brothers named the troublesome stretch "Christmas Rapid." Arriving at the mouth of Diamond Creek on January 4, they hiked up the tributary canyon to Peach Springs to obtain supplies for the remainder of the voyage. On January 8, they returned to the river, proceeded down the canyon by the Grand Wash Cliffs on January 13 and on to Needles where they arrived on January 18, one hundred and one days after their embarkation at Green River. The brothers were the twenty-sixth and twenty-seventh individuals to complete a boat trip through the Grand Canyon.

The motion picture film taken during their voyage was shown in their studio at the South Rim and established a record for being the longest continuously billed presentation of a commercial film.

In commenting on their trip, the Kolbs were guilty of a severe misjudgement when they wrote, "The trip is unusual and will hardly become a popular tour." In 1972, 16,432 people made the trip through the Grand Canyon.

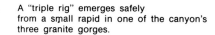
A "triple rig" emerges safely from a small rapid in one of the canyon's three granite gorges.

Ellsworth authored a book entitled *Through the Grand Canyon from Wyoming to Mexico* which was published in 1914 and has been reprinted several times, the volume becoming a classic in literature of the American Southwest and river running.

The brothers later traveled throughout the country, lecturing and showing photographs of the river voyage and the Grand Canyon. Their activities did much to acquaint the public with the beauty of the region and helped promote tourism to the canyon.

In 1921, Ellsworth was the head boatman for a mapping and dam survey of Cataract Canyon by the U. S. Geological Survey and the Southern California Edison Company. Emery aided as a boatman and photographer. Emery was the head boatman for the U. S. G. S. Grand Canyon expedition in 1923.

Emery acquired Ellsworth's interest in the photographic studio when Ellsworth moved to California in 1924. Ellsworth died in 1960 and is buried in the Grand Canyon Village cemetery.

In 1969, the centennial year of the Powell expedition, a banquet was held to honor Emery for his activities on the Colorado River and at the Grand Canyon. The Governor of Arizona delivered the principal address.

In 1974, at the age of 93, Emery made a two-day Grand Canyon river trip from the mouth of the Little Colorado to below Crystal Rapid. Flown to the junction of the Colorado and the Little Colorado, Kolb boarded a 37-foot long inflated raft provided by Grand Canyon Expeditions for the voyage. Also on the trip was the remarkable river historian, Otis "Dock" Marston, then 80 years old. Below Crystal Rapid, Kolb left the canyon by helicopter, while Marston continued on through the canyon to Pearce Ferry.

In May, 1976, Kolb and Marston made an airplane trip from the South Rim into the canyon and upriver to Marble Canyon Lodge below Lee's Ferry. On the flight, they proceeded up a branch of Nankoweap Canyon to see Kolb Natural Bridge, the largest natural bridge in the Grand Canyon. It was first discovered in 1871, but forgotten until 1953, when U. S. Senator Barry M. Goldwater, rediscovered the bridge while flying over the canyon.

Canyoneer Emery Clifford Kolb, nearing the grand age of 96, ran his last rapid on the morning of December 11, 1976. A physically small man, he became a towering figure at the canyon. He made many impressions on the giant chasm — photographer and artist, explorer and river-runner, canyon enthusiast and advocate, lecturer and businessman, and longtime South Rim resident. The spirit and achievements of this extraordinary man will forever be a part of the Grand Canyon.

Bert Loper's Continuing River Career.

Bert Loper's encounters with the Colorado River and the Grand Canyon did not stop when he failed to re-unite with his comrades, Russell and Monett, on their 1907-08 canyon voyage. In 1914, Loper again joined Charles Russell in a boating venture for the purpose of making still photographs and a motion picture. When Russell's boat was lost in Cataract Canyon, the journey ended. In 1921, Loper acted as head boatman for the U. S. Geological Survey expedition on the San Juan River and during the next year, served in the same capacity for the Geological Survey trip on the upper Green. He hoped to be head boatman on the Survey's 1923 trip through the Grand Canyon, but was rejected in favor of Emery Kolb. Loper then became occupied, for the most part, on boat trips in the Glen Canyon Area. Finally, in 1939, when almost seventy years old, he made a run of the Grand Canyon and became one of the first hundred to complete the voyage.

Loper began another run of the Grand Canyon on July 7, 1949. At this time, he was less than a month away from his 80th birthday and suffering from serious heart trouble. The embarkation point was Lee's Ferry. Loper was accompanied by seven people and the party employed three boats and a rubber raft. With Loper in his home-made 18-foot boat was Wayne Nichol. Following lunch on the second day, Loper led the party into 24½ Mile Rapid and as his boat encountered the rough water, the aged river man was apparently struck with a heart attack. The uncontrolled boat capsized with Loper and Nichol being thrown into the water. Loper floated downriver, his life preserver keeping his head above water, but no efforts to swim were apparent. Nichol was able to climb onto the capsized boat, ride it for a distance and then swim to shore.

The saddened voyagers searched along the river for Loper and his boat. Although the boat was recovered seventeen miles below the site of the upset, Loper's body could not be found. The boat was pulled ashore and left as a memorial, an oar placed upright in a rock cairn. On the oar was the inscription: "Bert Loper, the Grand Old Man of the Colorado, born July 31, 1869; Died in 24½-Mile Rapid."

Loper expressed a desire to die on the river and be buried on its banks. For nearly twenty-six years he rested by the Colorado, but a hiker found some bleached bones near Cardenas Creek which were later identified as the remains of Bert Loper. The bones were removed from the canyon and buried at a Salt Lake City cemetery beside the body of his wife, Rachel.

The U. S. G. S. Survey.

In 1923, the U. S. Geological Survey conducted a boating expedition through the Grand Canyon for the purpose of surveying the river, the last stretch to be surveyed in detail. The survey began at Lee's Ferry with a party of ten men, an eleventh member was added at Bright Angel Creek. Colonel Claude Hale Birdseye organized and led the expedition. Emery Kolb was the head boatman.

In addition to its boats, food, surveying equipment and maps; the expedition carried still and motion picture cameras, film and the first radio to be taken into the canyon.

While camped below Soap Creek Rapid, members of the expedition heard the radio broadcast announcing the death of President Warren G. Harding. The party stopped at the head of a rapid at Point Hansbrough, camp was made opposite the point and the men spent August 10 in observance of the President's funeral. The rapid is now named President Harding Rapid.

Nearly 150 miles downriver from Lee's Ferry, Kolb's boat capsized in an unnamed rapid. The event provided the rough water with the name, Upset Rapid.

On October 13, topographic engineer Roland Burchard connected his survey line with an upriver line he had run in 1920 and the survey was completed. Burchard had run an unbroken plane-table traverse and level line 252 miles from Lee's Ferry with only a 9-foot gross error in elevation.

A natural arch on the left bank of the river near the point where the two surveys join is named Triumphal Arch, commemorating the successful completion of the Grand Canyon Survey.

An obstacle to travel,
a horrid abyss,
or the most sublime creation of nature;
how one feels about the Grand Canyon is a simple matter of perspective.

The Disappearance of Glen and Bessie Hyde.

Glen R. Hyde was a twenty-eight year old native of Idaho who had navigated Idaho's Salmon River and the Peace and Fraser Rivers in Canada. In the Spring of 1928, he married Bessie, a twenty-four year old Parkersburg, West Virginia girl. Their honeymoon was to be a boating excursion through the Grand Canyon.

Hyde built their craft at Green River, Utah, a Salmon River type scow equipped with two sweep oars, fore and aft.

They left Green River on October 20, 1928 carrying along as a guide a copy of Ellsworth Kolb's book *Through the Grand Canyon from Wyoming to Mexico.* Although life preservers were absent from their equipment, the couple boated down the Green to its confluence with the Colorado and on through Cataract Canyon without mishap. Bessie thus became the first woman to make a transit of Cataract Canyon and its many rapids.

They navigated Glen Canyon, passed Lee's Ferry and proceeded into the Marble Gorge of the Grand Canyon. On November 15, twenty-six days after they had embarked, the bride and groom arrived at Bright Angel Creek. Mooring their scow, Glen and Bessie hiked to the South Rim where Emery Kolb entertained them at his rim home and listened to their story. Kolb vigorously urged that the couple take along life preservers for the continuation of their voyage, but they refused. This was a dreadful decision which undoubtedly cost Glen and Bessie their lives.

Some evidence suggested that Bessie did not wish to continue the trip, but the honeymooners did return to their scow and set out from Bright Angel Creek on November 17. They were last seen some seven miles downriver at Hermit Rapid.

Because no word was received from the couple for some time, Glen's father hurriedly left Idaho for the canyon's South Rim. He asked the National Park Service and the Army for assistance in finding his son and daughter-in-law and contracted with two men to conduct a boating search along the river. The men boated from Bright Angel Creek to Diamond Creek without finding a trace of the missing couple. A telegram requesting assistance in the search was sent to Emery Kolb who was in Phoenix preparing to undergo an appendectomy. Kolb returned to the canyon without his surgery.

Meanwhile, a two-man Army crew from March Field in California had flown up the canyon and sighted a boat. Emery Kolb was flown over the site and the boat was identified as the Hyde's scow. Kolb placed its location several miles below Diamond Creek, in the lower stretch of the Grand Canyon. He then organized a trip designed to reach the scow.

Emery had heard rumors that there was an old flat-bottomed boat at Diamond Creek so he took some oars, equipment and supplies and with Hyde's father and Park Ranger James Brooks set out to meet his brother Ellsworth who had been recruited to assist in the search. Emery's party rendezvoused with Ellsworth at Peach Springs which is located at the head of the road that leads to Diamond Creek. From Peach Springs, the group proceeded to the mouth of Diamond Creek where the old boat was found and repaired. The Kolb brothers and Ranger Brooks then began their search downriver.

Hyde's father walked seven miles upriver from Diamond Creek looking for some sign of the missing couple. He found some footprints, but none were seen at Diamond Creek.

Pages 70 and 71.
"At 6:15 p.m. I ran up to the verge of the Canyon and had my first memorable and overwhelming view in the light and shade of the setting sun. It is the most tremendous expression of erosion and the most ornate and complicated I ever saw. Man seeks the finest marbles for sculptures; Nature takes cinders, ashes, sediments, and makes all divine in fineness of beauty—turrets, towers, pyramids, battlemented castles, rising in glowing beauty from the depths of this canyon of canyons noiselessly hewn from the smooth mass of the featureless plateau."
John Muir, 1896, upon viewing the Grand Canyon of the Colorado River.

Stone Creek Falls.

The Kolbs and Ranger Brooks came upon the scow near Mile 237, eleven miles below Diamond Creek. The boat was right side up with some 14 inches of water in the bottom. It was held by a line which had hooked on rocks underwater. The line was cut and the scow pulled to shore. Bessie's diary, camera and several other valuable items were found, but there were no clues as to the whereabouts of the missing couple.

The cause of the Hydes' mysterious disappearance has never been established. Information about their trip below Hermit Rapid was logged in Bessie's diary which revealed that they passed Tapeats Creek on November 22. On the 30th, Bessie noted that they had run sixteen rapids. Forty-two notches were cut into the scow's gunwale evidently representing one for each day of the voyage.

Several theories have been offered to explain the couple's fate. Emery Kolb felt a plausible explanation was that Bessie was holding the scow by a line while Glen examined a rapid, but she was pulled into the river and Glen made an attempt to save her and both were drowned.

It is also possible that the scow broke away from its moorings leaving the pair stranded in a location from which they could not escape. As a consequence, the Hydes may have died from exposure to winter weather, from starvation, or both.

Another theory suggested that the scow hit some rocks on the right bank of the river at 232 Mile Rapid and the Hydes were thrown into the river where, without life preservers, and with another rapid a short distance below, they drowned.

What really happened to the bride and groom is not known except that their unique honeymoon, a river voyage through the Grand Canyon led to their untimely deaths.

At dusk, the canyon often glows with the serenity of a soft inner light.

The scarlet blossom of a solitary monkey flower punctuates
a tiny world of fern greenery in Fern Glen Canyon.

Lava Falls.

First Solo Run of the Canyon.

Haldane "Buzz" Holstrom became the first to make a solo
run through the Grand Canyon. His voyage was made in fifty
two days and ended at Hoover Dam on Thanksgiving Day,
November 25, 1937.

"Buzz" later said, "My first impression when I hit the lake
(Mead) was one of relief. I thought 'Hurrah! my troubles are all
over now,' but you know something, that sentiment didn't last
very long before it was replaced by an empty feeling; it was as
though everything I had ever striven for so long had been
accomplished and there was nothing left to do."

He further said about his unique voyage, "It was well worth
everything it cost me in time, money, and the rest. It seems like
I actually lived more in a few hours out there on the river than I
have in a year in the city."

The following year, Holstrom made a second trip, this time
accompanied by Amos Burg who ran the first rubber raft
through the canyon. The raft was sixteen feet long, five and a
half feet wide, and weighed only 83 pounds.

There were other early water transits of the Grand Canyon. In 1927, Clyde Eddy led a voyage and in 1934, Eddy was a member of a trip facetiously called the "Dusty Dozen." The California Institute of Technology conducted an expedition in 1937. There were also many shorter boat trips along different stretches of the canyon.

Commercial River Operations and Power Boats in the Canyon.

Commercial river running in the Grand Canyon started in 1938 with trips offered by Norman Davies Nevills of Mexican Hat in southeastern Utah. Nevills' initial trip which consisted of six people and three boats began at Green River, Utah on June 20. Accompanying Nevills and two boatmen were William C. Gibson, Lois Jotter and Elzada Urseba Clover. Miss Clover was a botanist and on the faculty of the University of Michigan and Miss Jotter a student at the University. The trip had been organized so that they might acquire plant collections along the Green and Colorado Rivers. Clover and Jotter became the first women to make a water transit of the Grand Canyon and were also among the first to study the botanical aspects along the canyons of the two rivers. They later authored a report about this study.

In 1940, Nevills made his second commercial Grand Canyon trip which began at Green River, Wyoming on June 20. When the party reached Green River, Utah, Barry Goldwater, who later became a senator from Arizona and was the Republican party's 1964 presidential nominee, joined and remained with the trip to its end on August 20. Goldwater and other party members are on the roster of the first hundred through the canyon by water.

In all, Nevills made seven Grand Canyon trips before he and his wife were killed when their airplane crashed after takeoff at Mexican Hat. Their ashes were scattered over the Grand Canyon.

1942 marked the initial canyon voyage of Otis "Dock" Marston of Berkeley, California who became a Grand Canyon boatman and eminent Colorado River system historian. Marston served as an oarsman on Nevills' canyon runs in 1947 and 1948 and in 1949 piloted the first powerboat down the canyon. In 1960, Marston was a member of the crew to make the first complete up canyon powerboat expedition.

Motorboating in the Grand Canyon began with attempts to go upriver. In the 1940's, Harry LeRoy Aleson made several runs into the lower canyon and eventually penetrated sixty miles upriver to Mile 218, eight miles above Diamond Creek. In 1914, he ran his powerboat to Mile 221 where he struck a rock, wrecking the motor's lower unit.

In June, 1948, Ed Hudson attempted an upriver run hoping to cover the entire canyon to Lee's Ferry. Hudson and marine architect William Garden designed a Higgins-type craft which was named the *Esmeralda II* after the first steamboat to reach the head of steamer navigation on the lower Colorado, but the boat did not have sufficient power to negotiate 217 Mile Rapid.

The following year, Hudson changed his direction and organized a downriver trip. He replaced the engine with a more powerful 125-horsepower motor and the first motorpowered

Pages 73, 74 and 75. Lava Falls, noted as the most perilous rapid in the Grand Canyon was usually portaged by early river-runners, but the equipment used by most of today's river men makes it possible, for any one who might so wish, to "enjoy" the journey over and through this extent of white water. The pictures on pages 73, 74 and 75 give an account of one boating party's brief encounter with the master rapid of the Grand Canyon.

The Vishnu Temple at sunset.
Vishnu, the preserver and protector of the world,
is one of three godheads belonging to the Hindu trinity.
Brahma, the creator and Shiva, the destroyer are the other two figures of the trinity.

Pages 78 and 79.
The Grand Canyon of the Colorado River from Hopi Point.

trip from Lee's Ferry to Pearce Ferry was accomplished between June 12 and June 17. All the rapids in the canyon were run with Hance Rapid at Mile 76.5 being the most difficult.

"Dock" Marston made eight hard-hulled motorboat transits of the canyon during the 1950's and served as the technical advisor to the Walt Disney Studio during the production of a fictionalized motion picture of Major Powell's 1869 voyage. In 1969, Marston, then 75 years old, rowed a seven-foot plastic Sportyak on a low water trip through the canyon. The craft is on display at the Visitor Center on the South Rim.

In 1959, Indiana Gear Works, a manufacturer of jet water pump units for propulsion of boats in shallow water, organized an up canyon run. Their two fiberglass Turbocraft boats equipped with jet units could not proceed beyond Mile 234; however, the company decided to make another attempt the following year. "Dock" Marston was retained as an advisor and it was decided to make a downriver run first to cache food and fuel for the upriver endeavor.

Due to cold weather in the Rocky Mountains, the water level in the river was low. This condition greatly increased the chance of striking rocks and the situation was further complicated by the boats being heavily loaded. About three miles below Lee's Ferry, one boat struck a rock causing damage to its hull. Though the boat was repaired, that night, Marston later recalled "was one of my toughest nights ever on the river, I was awake all night. I got up in the morning and said, 'Okay, we're going back to Lee's Ferry'" and he added, "one month from now we start again."

On Saturday, June 18, they again embarked from Lee's Ferry. There were four jet-propelled boats, two twenty-four feet long, the *Big Red* and *Big Yellow*, and two eighteen footers, the *Wee Red* and *Wee Yellow*.

At Lava Falls, on June 23, Marston was on board the *Big Red* operated by William Austin. Marston, who set the course through the tough rapid, later recalled, "We took off the top of that wave and we shot out into the air and I estimate we dropped ten feet. I could see that this was going to be a real jolt so I got way down, I was hanging on to the rope. . . it didn't bother my legs any but it did strain a muscle in my collar bone." Suddenly Austin pulled back on the throttle and the boat was without power in the middle of the raging rapid. Quietly he told Marston to take the controls; he had broken his left leg in the drop. Austin was taken to shore just below the rapid and Marston continued downriver to Whitmore Wash to send a message requesting air rescue. Early the next morning, an Air Force helicopter arrived to remove the injured boater. In reference to the accident, Marston later said "Now that's adventure, please keep it away from me!" The downriver run terminated at Boulder City.

The upriver assault began at Boulder City on July 3, 1960. All four of the boats were equipped with inboard engines, two (*Wee Red* and *Wee Yellow*) rated at 184 horsepower and the other two (*Kiwi* and *Dock*) at 188 horsepower.

The expedition encountered its first real difficulty at Lava Falls which, with a drop of thirty-seven feet, is rated as the Grand Canyon's most severe rapid. On July 5, the *Kiwi* was driven through the rapid by Jon Hamilton, a New Zealander. After several unsuccesful attempts, Hamilton piloted the *Wee Red* and *Wee Yellow* through the falls and on the evening of July 6, after ten aborted attempts, he captained the *Dock* to the top of Lava.

The *Wee Yellow* was damaged in an ascent of Dubendorff Rapid and was lost when, on the morning of July 10, it dropped into a hole in Grapevine Rapid and sank in approximately forty seconds.

The remaining three boats reached Lee's Ferry on the afternoon of July 12, completing the first upriver transit of the Grand Canyon.

On Easter Sunday, April 10, 1955, twenty-six year old William Beer and twenty-seven year old John Daggett waded into the water at Lee's Ferry and began probably the most unusual water transit of the Grand Canyon, a 279 mile swim to Pearce Ferry at Lake Mead. They completed their unique trip after 26 days, having, with exception of Hance, negotiated all of the river's rapids. On a later boat trip through the canyon, Beer swam Hance.

Following the Powell expedition in 1869, boat travel through the canyon was slow in developing and eighty years elapsed before the one hundredth individual completed the trip. With the advent of commercial river-running companies, trips increased and the next five years saw the second hundred voyagers complete the Grand Canyon transit by water. Substantial growth in river tourism increased until 1972 when the peak of 16,432 "river-runners" was reached. The National Park Service, concerned with the possible adverse effects the traffic might have on the environment, placed a limit on the number of people allowed to make the canyon trip in one year. Following the establishment of this limit, the number has decreased.

Today, commercial river-running companies are almost entirely responsible for providing transportation, equipment and guide services for those who would like to see the Grand Canyon from a Colorado River vantage.

Legislation and the National Park.

In 1882, Senator Benjamin Harrison of Indiana, later to become President of the United States, introduced a bill in Congress to set aside the Grand Canyon as the nation's second national park. Yellowstone had, in 1872, become the first to be so designated. Harrison's bill was not acted upon and two other bills which he introduced in 1883 and 1886 also failed to pass. When Harrison became president he proclaimed the Grand Canyon Forest Reserve, closing the area to homesteading, but continuing to allow mining.

President Theodore Roosevelt signed a bill in 1906 which created the Grand Canyon Game Reserve, affording protection to game animals, but not their predators. New mining claims in the canyon area were prohibited with the establishment in 1908 of the Grand Canyon National Monument.

Unsuccessful bills to create Grand Canyon National Park were introduced in 1910 and 1911. Arizona became a state in 1912 and bills to form the park were sponsored in 1917 by the state's Representative Carl Hayden and Senator Henry Fountain Ashurst. Finally, on February 26, 1919; thirty-seven years after Harrison's initial attempt, President Woodrow Wilson signed the bill creating Grand Canyon National Park.

In 1927, changes were made to the park's boundaries, one major change being the addition of the Kaibab forest land on the North Rim. By 1974, the physical dimensions of the park measured approximately fifty-six miles long and twenty-two miles wide. In 1975, the boundary was again changed. Some areas were added and some land deleted and made a part of the Havasupai Indian Reservation.

On December 22, 1932, President Herbert C. Hoover's proclamation established a second Grand Canyon National Monument (Toroweap), the first having become Grand Canyon National Park. In 1975, the second Grand Canyon National Monument was merged into the park. This new land included in the park was essentially on the north side of the Colorado River.

Marble Canyon National Monument was established by the presidential proclamation of Lyndon B. Johnson on January 20, 1969. The monument, stretching along the 52 miles of the Marble Gorge to the northern boundary of Grand Canyon National Park was incorporated into the park in 1975.

THE LIVING CANYON

The Colorado Plateau is centered in the Four Corners region of the United States where the boundaries of Arizona, New Mexico, Utah and Colorado meet. It is distinguished from adjoining areas by its high altitude which averages more than 5000 feet above sea level, by extensive areas of nearly horizontal sedimentary rocks through which deep and steep walled canyons have been cut, by great expanses of barren rock and by an arid climate with sparse vegetation. Approximately ninety percent of the plateau's 130,000 square miles is drained by the Colorado River.

Rising in north central Colorado and emptying into the Gulf of California, the Colorado River is approximately 1450 miles in length. The Colorado's principal tributary is the Green River, originating in the Wind River Mountains of Wyoming and joining the Colorado at the Confluence in Canyonlands National Park.

Situated in the southwestern part of the Colorado Plateau, the Grand Canyon is the longest and deepest of the many canyons carved by the Colorado River.

The length of the Grand Canyon is 277.4 miles from its beginning below the Vermilion and Echo Cliffs in northern Arizona to its terminus at the Grand Wash Cliffs. Mileage through the canyon is measured from Lee's Ferry which has been designated as Mile 0 although, in fact, Lee's Ferry is .3 of a mile above the actual inception of the canyon which occurs at the mouth of the Paria River.

Seven large plateaus border the canyon. Between Lee's Ferry and the mouth of the Little Colorado, the Marble Platform lies on both sides of the canyon. Downriver, six plateaus rim the canyon, four on the north side and two on the south. The northern plateaus are, from east to west, the Kaibab, Kanab, Unikaret and Shivwits. On the south side of the canyon are the Coconino to the east and the Hualapai to the west.

Below the mouth of the Paria River, the canyon walls form the Marble Gorge which extends down the Colorado 61.1 miles to the mouth of the Little Colorado River. The splendid, narrow, steep-walled gorge was mis-named "Marble Canyon" by John Wesley Powell who had mistaken water polished Redwall Limestone for marble. The term gorge is preferred to canyon.

Below the Marble Gorge are the Upper (Mile 77 to Mile 117.8), Middle (Mile 126.6 to Mile 130.5) and Lower (Mile 215.1 to Mile 277.7) Granite Gorges, which have been carved into the

Plants like this brightly blossomed
prickly pear cactus
are well adapted to the high temperatures
and sparse precipitation
found at low inner canyon elevations
where a desert climate is common.

The Colorado River and inner walls
of the Grand Canyon at Mile 157
near the mouth of Havasu Creek.

Every tiny streamlet
and each plant of the canyon
add to the forces of erosion
which work inexorably at carving
the singular world
that is the Grand Canyon.

Mount Hayden
and the distant Painted Desert
are pictured near Point Imperial
on the North Rim of the Grand Canyon.

Traveling to Cape Royal,
one passes through the green world
of the Walhalla Plateau,
but rounding a corner
and descending a hill,
this view of the canyon opens.
To the right,
obscured by shadow is
the Angel's Window, a natural bridge eroded out
of the North Rim's Kaibab Limestone.
A short foot trail starting
at the Cape Royal parking area
leads on to the Angel's Window
providing excellent canyon vistas.

The Claret-Cup Cactus.

dark, hard Precambrian schists and gneisses which are interspersed with dikes and sills of granitic material.

At Lee's Ferry the Colorado River is approximately 3107 feet above sea level..The river descends approximately 1878 feet through the Grand Canyon to Lake Mead where, although the elevation of the lake's surface fluctuates, a maximum of 1229 feet above sea level is planned. The average drop of the river is 7.9 feet per mile, or approximately 25 times greater than that of the Mississippi.

About fifty percent of the river descent occurs at abrupt rapids which constitute only nine percent of the canyon's length. Twenty percent of this fall takes place in just 20 of the 161 recognized rapids which occur in the Grand Canyon. The velocity of the river in smooth water is roughly four miles per hour, while in rapids, it varies between seven and a half and ten miles per hour.

The river's average depth is approximately fifty feet; the deepest measured spot is at Mile 114.3, where the river reaches a depth of 110 feet.

Generally, the river's width varies between 200 and 300 feet. The narrowest spot is located in the Granite Narrows, a one mile long Precambrian rock gorge which begins at Mile 135.1. There, canyon walls squeeze the river down to an approximate width of sixty feet.

Prior to the closing of the gates of Glen Canyon Dam in 1963, the flow of the river varied from less than 1000 cubic feet per second to a recorded high, in 1884, of 325,000 cubic feet per second. Today, because of the control placed on the river by Glen Canyon Dam, the median discharge is 12,200 cubic feet per second. However, in comparison to other major rivers of the United States, the Colorado does not have a large flow of water. The water volume of the Colorado River is only 5 to 10 percent of that carried by the Ohio, Missouri, Snake or Columbia Rivers.

Before the installation of Glen Canyon Dam, the Colorado transported an average sediment load of 143 million tons per year through the Grand Canyon. In 1927, four hundred eighty million tons were carried with 27,600,000 tons in only one day. The dam's construction has minimized the sediment load passing through the canyon thus giving some credence to the predictions that the canyon's sand beaches will disappear.

There are 161 rapids in the Grand Canyon, but this number varies according to the water flow, the lower the flow the more rapids. Formation of the majority of these rapids has been caused by rock debris deposited in the river at the mouths of side canyons, but many have occurred where blocks of rock have fallen from the canyon walls or where there is a resistant outcropping of rock. Lava Falls is of the latter origin. Rapids have also formed where bars of gravel accumulations have been found.

The severity of rapids for navigation is measured on a scale of 1 to 10. A rating of 1 indicates a riffle, 2 and 3, light rapids, 4 to 6, medium rapids and 7 through 10, heavy rapids. A high water flow generally diminishes or, in some cases, can eliminate a rapid. For example, Sockdolager Rapid in the Upper Granite Gorge disappears at flows of 60,000 cubic feet per second.

There are twenty-six major rapids in the Grand Canyon which are rated from 5 to 10. Nine are found in the sixty-one miles of the Marble Gorge, six are located between the mouth of the Little Colorado River and Phantom Ranch and eleven from Phantom Ranch to Lake Mead.

The elevation at Grand Canyon Village on the South Rim is 6860 feet and at Hopi Point, 7071 feet while at Point Imperial on the North Rim, the altitude is 8803 feet. The lowest point in the canyon is at the head of Lake Mead, where the altitude is 1175 feet. The canyon is over one mile deep at several points along either rim.

Between Grand Canyon Village, on the South Rim, and Grand Canyon Lodge, on the North Rim, the canyon's width is about eleven miles. Across canyon from Desert View to Cape Final, the distance is eight miles, the same as the width separating Hermit's Rest from Point Sublime. At some locations, the canyon rims narrow to a separation of less than 1000 feet. Navajo Bridge which traverses the Marble Gorge near Lee's Ferry is 834 feet long.

The bottom of the Grand Canyon has a desert climate with an average annual precipitation of slightly under ten inches. Twenty-nine percent of the annual precipitation occurs in July and August when thunderstorms are common. May is the driest month of the year having only 3.4 percent of the annual precipitation, while April and June each receive 5.6 percent.

On the canyon floor, the yearly average temperature is 68° F. High summer temperatures are common, the mean maximum for June is 101° F., July 106° F. and August 103° F. December, the coldest month, has an average temperature of 40° F. at Phantom Ranch.

At many intermediate canyon levels such as the Tonto Platform, the climate is semi-arid, with annual precipitation varying between ten and twenty-five inches. Snow fall is light.

A highland climate occupies the cool and moist areas along and behind the higher canyon rims. The average annual precipitation on the Kaibab Plateau exceeds twenty-five inches, much of which is in the form of snow fall. The North Rim's average yearly snow fall is twelve and a half feet.

At Grand Canyon Village on the South Rim, yearly precipitation is approximately fifteen and a half inches, with an average annual snowfall of five feet.

Average maximum and minimum temperatures on the North Rim are 56° F. and 30° F. respectively, while at the South Rim averages are 62° F. for the high and 35° F. for the low.

July, the warmest month, has a mean maximum temperature of 77° F. on the North Rim and 84° F. on the South Rim. January, the coldest month, has a mean minimum temperature of 16° F. at the North Rim and 18° F. at the South Rim.

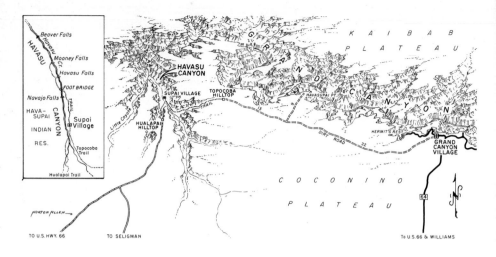

Havasu Falls.

The Havasupai Indians are the only Indians presently living
in the Grand Canyon. Their village, Supai, is located in Havasu Canyon
and is approximately 34 air miles northwest of Grand Canyon Village,
2500 feet below the rim of the Grand Canyon.
The village is not directly reached by road, but two unimproved roads
do terminate at rims of canyons tributary to Havasu Canyon and foot trails
descend each side canyon to Havasu Canyon and Supai. For information
concerning these roads and trails, contact the National Park Service.
Havasu Creek, a beautiful blue-green stream, rises at a spring
approximately one and one-half miles up-canyon from Supai
and imparts an oasis like character to its sheer, red rock walled canyon
as it flows to its confluence with the Colorado River.
The color of the stream comes from salts in solution and gives
the Havasupai their name which means "people of the blue-green water."
In its course to join the Colorado River,
Havasu Creek plunges over three spectacular waterfalls.
Navajo Falls, with a drop of approximately 75 feet,
is located only one and one-half miles below Supai and was named for
Chief Navajo, a Havasupai leader who died in 1898.
Havasu Falls, with its drop of 100 feet and graceful travertine terraces,
is considered one of the most scenic waterfalls in all the world.
The falls have also been called "Bridal Veil Falls"
and are only one-half mile below Navajo Falls.
At Mooney Falls, one mile below Havasu Falls,
Havasu Creek hurtles 196 feet over a sheer drop creating the highest waterfall
in Havasu Canyon. The falls are named for James Mooney,
a prospector who died in 1879 while attempting to descend to the bottom
of Havasu Canyon near the site of the falls.
Beaver Falls is a small waterfall or rapid located about six miles
below Supai. The falls were named for beaver
that once inhabited Havasu Canyon.

Havasu Canyon.

The range in climates at the Grand Canyon provides many biologic environments with extensive varieties of plants and animals. More than 1000 different kinds of flowering plants occur in the canyon.

The native plant and animal life of the Grand Canyon is divided into six major biotic communities. A biotic community is an assemblage of plants and animals living in a particular physical habitat. Biotic communities are not exclusive and plants and animals of one community may be found in another.

Within the canyon, the Riparian Biotic Community is situated along the Colorado River and lower portions of its tributaries. Prominent among the Riparian plants are Fremont cottonwoods, horsetails, tamarix, and Red, Coyote and Seep willows.

Cottonwoods attain heights approaching 115 feet and a single tree may use more than fifty gallons of water per day. Many of the cottonwoods growing at Phantom Ranch were planted by David D. Rust when he operated Rust's Camp, a fore-runner to Phantom Ranch.

Tamarix, also called salt cedar, is native to the Mediterranean area, but was introduced into the United States in the early 1800's. The plant has spread along numerous water courses and into moist areas in the Southwest where it forms a dense, jungle-like growth along the banks of many rivers and streams. It is the most common plant along the Colorado River, but its undesirable trait of consuming large amounts of ground water while displacing native growth have, during the last forty years, caused Tamarix to become a serious nuisance.

Mammals living in the Riparian Community include ringtail cats, spotted skunks, river otters, beaver, rock pocket mice, and long tailed pocket mice.

The canyon wren and large black raven are common birds along the river while the beautiful great blue heron is often seen standing at the river's edge.

The Kaibab squirrel,
an endangered resident of the Grand Canyon's North Rim
forests of ponderosa pines, is now almost extinct.

The Colorado River squawfish, largest member of the minnow family, is endemic to the river as are the humpback sucker and the bonytail chub, Trout are found in several perennial tributaries to the Colorado.

Several species of reptiles, including the unique pink colored Grand Canyon rattlesnake, occur along the banks of the river while a few amphibian species survive in moist areas of the canyon bottom.

The most extensive biotic community in the canyon is the Desertscrub Biotic Community which occurs in the inner gorges, on the Tonto Platform and at other intermediate canyon levels.

The principal plant of the community is blackbrush. Other plants include Mormon tea, segolily, honey mesquite, sand verbena, beaver tail cactus, narrow leaf yucca, dollarpoint prickly pear, cataclaw, desert trumpet, desert thorn, Utah agave, desert prince's plume, pale evening primrose, white bursage, ocotilla, cholla and barrel cactus.

Among the Desertscrub mammals are the spectacular bighorn sheep, coyotes, Gunnison's prairie dogs, ringtail cats, rock squirrels, black tailed jack rabbits, spotted skunks, cliff chipmunks, cactus mice, canyon mice and spotted ground squirrels.

Also living in the Desertscrub and Riparian Communities are the Grand Canyon's wild burros. The animals are frequently seen along the river, especially in the western canyon. The burro, a native of northeast Africa, was brought to North America in the 16th Century by the Spanish and to the Grand Canyon by prospectors and miners who, upon leaving, often simply turned their animals loose.

Where burros habitually range, the vegetative abundance has declined approximately twenty percent and the number of plant species has diminished about fifty percent. Soil erosion has accelerated in areas heavily grazed by burros.

As a result of this serious damage caused to the canyon's Desertscrub and Riparian Communities, between 1924 and 1969, the National Park Service eliminated about 3000 burros; however, adverse public sentiment caused the Park Service to abandon this policy.

The Pinon-Juniper Biotic Community is found along and behind both the North and South Rims. The pinon pine, with its edible nuts, and the Utah juniper give the community its name.

Other principal plants of the Pinon-Juniper region include cliff rose, Mormon tea, serviceberry, broadleaf yucca, blackbrush and rabbitbrush. Among the animals are mule deer, desert cottontails, cliff chipmunks, gray foxes, Stephen's wood rats, violet-green swallows, ravens, white-throated swifts, Clark nutcrackers, pinon jays and scrub jays. Mountain lions may occasionally wander into this region.

The Pinon-Juniper grades into the Yellow Pine Biotic Community. The yellow pine, also called ponderosa pine, is an important lumber tree. The forest grows at elevations which range from about 7000 feet to 8200 feet above sea level.

The Yellow Pine forestland includes Gambel's oaks, locust, creeping mahonia, mountain mahogany and blue elderberry.

Animals of the community include some of special interest to the Grand Canyon. The rare white-tailed Kaibab squirrel is found only in the ponderosa forest of the North Rim where he lives in close association with the ponderosa pines, using the trees as nesting sites and the pine seeds as food. The Abert and Kaibab squirrels are close relatives; but the Abert, unlike his relative, is more widely distributed and is found in various localities in the Southwest, including the South Rim of the Grand Canyon.

Other mammals found in the Yellow Pine Community include striped skunks, which are frequently seen at Grand Canyon Village especially around El Tovar Hotel, deer, porcupines, golden mantled ground squirrels, Mexican wood rats, Nuttall's cottontails, Merriam's shrews and Uinta chipmunks.

A beautiful Spruce-Fir Biotic Community is situated high on the North Rim at altitudes above 8200 feet where the environment is characterized by cold weather, heavy snow fall and a short growing season. Trees living in this community include Engelmann spruce, blue spruce, Douglas fir, white fir, aspen and mountain ash. Mammals of the Spruce-Fir forest include red squirrels, porcupines, Uinta chipmunks and northern pocket gophers. Wild turkeys are often seen parading among the trees and on the meadows.

Several lovely meadows dot the Spruce-Fir Community of the North Rim. These shallow, open areas constitute the Mountain Grass Land Community with a wildlife population which includes voles, gophers, weasels, chipmunks and wild turkeys.

Mule deer are found throughout the biotic communities of the canyon, but they are particularly common within the Yellow Pine and Spruce-Fir Forests. Because of a disastrous early conservation attempt on the North Rim, deer of the Kaibab Plateau gained prominence in the annals of ecological history when, in 1906, before the National Park was created, the Grand Canyon Game Reserve was established to protect game animals, but not their predators. James T. "Uncle Jim" Owens was appointed warden and, over the next twelve years, exterminated approximately 500 mountain lions. Owens is reported to have placed a sign near his cabin which read, "Lions Caught to Order, Reasonable Rates." Hunting parties additionally reduced the mountain lion population while other predators, including coyotes, bobcats, wolves and bears were also killed.

Originally, approximately 4000 deer inhabited the North Rim, but with the disappearance of natural predators, the herd experienced explosive growth and by 1924 had erupted to some 100,000 members. The North Rim soon became severely over-grazed and the environment was unable to support the large deer population.

As a consequence, a deer drive was organized that was hoped would alleviate the overpopulation. The drive would move several thousand animals from the North Rim, across the canyon, to the South Rim. The planned route was down the Nankoweap Trail to the Colorado River and up the Tanner Trail. Over one hundred men participated. However, the deer were uncooperative and the novel population redistribution effort met with failure.

Because of this over-population, almost 80,000 deer died between 1924 and 1930 while the following ten years brought an additional 10,000 deaths. Today, the North Rim deer herd is comprised of approximately 10,000 members, a number which seems to have come into balance with the environment.

CREATION OF THE GRAND CANYON LANDSCAPE

The earth is estimated to be almost five billion years old and from the loftiest point on its rims to the deepest recess of its gorge, the Grand Canyon provides an unexcelled view into the last two billion years of geological history and biological evolution of the Southwest.

The Early Precambrian Era.

The oldest rocks exposed in the Grand Canyon are found in the narrow V-shaped granite gorges at the bottom of the great chasm. These hard dark colored rocks date from the Early Precambrian, the oldest era of the geologic history of the earth. These ancient rocks were originally sand, mud and silt deposited in a sea about two billion years ago. Sediments may have accumulated to thicknesses which exceeded five miles, but the crust of the earth subsided as deposition occurred.

These deposits were compacted and cemented and formed into sedimentary rocks. Beginning about 1,700,000,000 years ago, they were uplifted into mountains during the Mazatzal Orogeny, a period of mountain building in Arizona.

The mountain building activity lasted between fifty to one hundred million years and exerted tremendous pressures and high temperatures on the sedimentary rocks. These great forces changed the sedimentary rocks into metamorphic rock types called schist and gneiss.

Within the mountains, molten rock worked its way upward through weak zones in the metamorphic rocks and as this material slowly cooled, it solidified into granite which has itself been chemically and physically altered as a result of exposure to metamorphic forces. Dikes and sills of white and pink colored metamorphosed granite are exposed in the dark gray to black schist and gneiss walls of the inner granite gorges.

Although the mountains attained high elevations, they were eventually worn to a low, near sea level topography called a peneplain.

The Late Precambrian Era.

Late in the Precambrian Era, older Precambrian rocks subsided and were covered by a shallow sea. More than 12,000 feet of sediments and volcanic rocks were deposited over older rocks. The sediments consolidated into limestones, shales, siltstones and conglomerates. The rocks were block-faulted and uplifted into the mountains. Rocks representative of the Late Precambrian mountains are recognized on top of the earlier Precambrian schists, gneisses and granites and are predominantly tilted about ten degrees to the northeast.

Plant fossils of both algae and fungi are present in some of these Late Precambrian rocks and are evidence of early types of life in the Grand Canyon region.

Over perhaps a period of 100 million years, these Late Precambrian mountains were eroded to a nearly flat surface. Approximately 12,000 feet of rock were stripped away and only remnants of the mountains remained. The erosional surface is called the Great Unconformity, a term which indicates a hiatus or gap in the geoligic record when erosion took place but no deposition occurred.

The Paleozoic Era.

The second major era of the earth's history, the Paleozoic, spans approximately 345 million years and is divided into seven periods. The oldest period of the Paleozoic Era is the Cambrian which began about 570 million years ago and ended 70 million years later.

"Marble Canon."
From Powell's "Exploration of the Colorado River of the West."

At the start of the Cambrian, a shallow sea advanced across the Grand Canyon area and sedimentary deposition formed the Tapeats Sandstone which is located above the Great Unconformity and on top of the tilted Late Precambrian rocks. The sandstone layer, 200 to 300 feet thick, is characterized by a nearly vertical brown layered cliff face. Small marine trilobites, possibly the first fossils of animals in the Grand Canyon, are found in the Tapeats Sandstone.

Above the Tapeats Sandstone is the Bright Angel Shale which is also of the Cambrian period and was deposited in the same sea. The shale is up to 450 feet thick and is grayish-green in color. It erodes quite easily and has been stripped off the surface of the underlying Tapeats Sandstone to form the Tonto Platform. Several types of fossils, including trilobites and brachiopods, are present.

Overlying the Bright Angel Shale is another rock layer from the Cambrian sea called the Muav Limestone. The Muav Limestone is about 350 feet thick, is gray and greenish-gray in color and contains fossil trilobites.

An erosional surface exists between the Muav Limestone and the next layer and is another unconformity. The Muav is of Cambrian age while the layer overlying, the Temple Butte Limestone, is dated in the late Devonian Period. Missing are two Paleozoic periods, the Ordovician and Silurian, which represent approxmately 95 to 115 million years.

The late Devonian Temple Butte is purplish-gray to pinkish-gray in color. In the eastern part of the canyon it is not a continuous layer, but is represented in isolated lenses, while in the western canyon it forms a continuous layer gradually increasing westward in thickness to over 1000 feet. A portion of the top of the limestone has eroded and its surface indicates that at one time a part of the depositional material of this period was above the surface of the sea. This erosional surface represents yet another unconformity.

Rock Formations	Approximate Thickness (Feet)	Landform	Depositional Environment	Description	Geologic Time Scale — Era	Geologic Time Scale — Period
Moenkopi Formation	400	Gentle Concave Slope	Tidal Flat	Remnants near the Grand Canyon; light red to dark brown colored, siltstones, shales, mudstones. Reptile tracks and trails.	Mesozoic	Triassic
Kaibab Limestone	300	Cliff	Marine	Light gray limestone, fossiliferous.	Paleozoic	Permian
Toroweap Formation	250	Cliff	Marine	Grayish limestone, beds of siltstone, mudstone, and sandstones. Fossiliferous.	Paleozoic	Permian
Coconino Sandstone	300	Cliff	Desert	Light tan cross bedded sandstone. Fossil tracks.	Paleozoic	Permian
Hermit Shale	300	Steep Slope	Savannah	Reddish shales, siltstones and mudstones. Plant fossils.	Paleozoic	Permian
Supai Group	900	Ledges and Slopes	Flood Plain	Reddish sandstones, shales, siltstones and limestones. Plant fossils and animal tracks.	Paleozoic	Permian and Pennsylvanian
Redwall Limestone	500	Cliff	Marine	Gray limestone stained red by overlying Hermit Shale and Supai sandstones. Marine fossils and solution caves.	Paleozoic	Mississippian
Temple Butte Limestone	30	Cliff	Marine	Purple to pinkish gray limestone. Few fossils.	Paleozoic	Devonian
Muav Limestone	600	Cliffs Ledges Slopes	Marine	Yellowish gray limestone and siltstone. Trilobite fossils and ripple marks.	Paleozoic	Cambrian
Bright Angel Shale	350-400	Low Slope Bench	Marine	Greenish gray shale. Trilobite and brachiopod fossils with tracks and trails of worms and trilobites.	Paleozoic	Cambrian
Tapeats Sandstone	100-300	Cliff	Marine	Coarse brown sandstone showing tracks of marine animals.	Paleozoic	Cambrian
Grand Canyon Super Group	Unknown	Slope	Marine	Sandstones, limestones, shales and siltstones.	Precambrian	Late
Vishnu Schist	Unknown	Steep Slope	Marine Metamorphism Molten Intrusions	Dark schists and gneisses intruded with white and pink granite dikes and sills.	Precambrian	Early

JFH

At least three extensive but shallow seas covered the Grand Canyon region during the Mississippian Period. Remnants of marine life in the seas formed a 500 feet thick layer of limestone now called the Redwall Limestone which is one of the most prominent cliff walls in the canyon. The formation is a very pure limestone and contains many marine fossils. Its true color is not red, but gray. The red coloring is a surface stain coming from the overlying Hermit Shale and Supai Group.

Because the limestone readily dissolves, many interesting topographic features have formed in it. These include arches, caves and the particularly large Redwall Cavern on the east bank of the Colorado River at Mile 33. Major John Wesley Powell estimated that if the cavern was utilized as a theater it could provide seating for 50,000 people.

About 280 million years ago, the climate of the earth became relatively arid. The Grand Canyon region; however, was still in a marine environment and rivers flowing from highlands northeast of the future canyon deposited sediments which became the Permian Period Supai Group, four red-colored formations, 700 to 1200 feet thick. The Supai sandstones form step-like slopes in the canyon and contain fossilized animal tracks and imprints of ferns.

Above the Supai is another Permian Period layer, the Hermit Shale. It forms a red to maroon colored slope and is between 200 and 900 feet in thickness. Many plant fossils have been found in the shale indicating it was formed in a semi-arid environment.

A conspicuous light tan colored vertical cliff rests on top of the reddish Hermit Shale. This prominent cliff is the Coconino Sandstone and can be easily traced along the canyon walls. It is 300 to 500 feet thick and represents sand deposited by winds blowing from the north when the Grand Canyon region was a desert. Approximately twenty-five different types of reptile fossil tracks have been identified in the Coconino formation.

Toward the end of the arid Permian Period, the Grand Canyon area was twice inundated by seas and the two uppermost formations of the canyon were deposited. Resting on the wind formed Coconino Sandstone is the marine Toroweap Formation with a depth ranging from 120 feet to more than 900 feet and above the Toroweap is the Kaibab Limestone which attains thicknesses of more than 800 feet.

The Kaibab Formation floors man's activities along the canyon rims. The limestone is grayish in color and marine fossils, including corals, brachiopods, sponges, snails, clams and fish teeth, have been discovered in the formation.

The Mesozoic Era.

The third major division in the geologic history of the earth is the Mesozoic Era which lasted 160 million years, from 225 to 65 million years ago. During this era, known as the Age of Dinosaurs, the Grand Canyon country experienced many different environments. It was invaded by seas, it was swampland and it was a desert.

The Cenozoic Era.

Some sixty-five million years ago, the present major division of geologic time, the Cenozoic Era, began. During this time, the Grand Canyon area was elevated high above sea level. As the vast plateau lands surrounding the present canyon were uplifted, the forces of erosion removed thousands of feet of the Mesozoic rocks. Prominent remnants of the Mesozoic rocks remain. East of Desert View is Cedar Mountain, about fifteen miles south of Grand Canyon Village is Red Butte and surrounding the canyon region on the east and north sides, the Echo and Vermilion Cliffs are composed of Mesozoic age rocks.

The rise of the land is explained by the theory of plate tectonics, or "Continental Drift." The crust, or lithosphere, of the earth is divided into several plates which slowly move over the underlying plastic asthenosphere. The plates are not permanent, but grow and are eventually destroyed. They form in areas called rises when basaltic magma moves upward from the interior of the earth. The magma joins existing plates along the rise. Plates are destroyed where they collide and one is underthrust in areas called trenches. Plate movement results in this process of plate growth and destruction and the consequent movement of continents on plates, "Continental Drift."

Most of the forty-nine continental United States are on the North American Plate. According to one theory, during the last sixty-five million years a large section of the western North American Plate, including the Grand Canyon area, was and is continuing to be elevated by the East Pacific Rise as the plate moves westward up and over the east flank of the rise. This theory is disputed by another hypothesis which contends that western North America is actually being rifted apart by divergent movements away from the rise.

The age and geologic history of the Colorado River and the Grand Canyon has been investigated by geologists for over a hundred years, but the chronology of geologic events associated with the cutting of the canyon by the river is still not known.

Several theories have been proposed for the excavation of the canyon. According to an early theory, the river originally flowed across a nearly level surface. As the land was uplifted, the river cut the canyon. This simple interpretation proved to be incorrect. Geologic evidence indicates the uplift predated the river in many cases. Apparently, different portions of the Colorado River have different ages and origins. Below the canyon, the river is approximately five million years old while upriver from the canyon its age is thirty to forty million years.

To reconcile the age discrepancy of the river above and below the canyon another theory was offered. According to this theory, the Colorado flowed in its present course through Utah into northern Arizona to the Little Colorado River. Then the Colorado followed the course of the the Little Colorado and eventually connected to the Rio Grande drainage, emptying into the Atlantic Ocean at the Gulf of Mexico. The theory additionally states that another river, smaller in size, flowed southwest from the plateau lands to the Gulf of California. This smaller river supposedly extended its head westward and captured the ancestral upper Colorado. As a consequence, a through flowing Colorado River was established and approximately 1,200,000 years ago, the Grand Canyon had been cut to within some fifty feet of its present depth.

A third theory disregards the idea of the ancestral upper Colorado flowing into the Gulf of Mexico via the Little Colorado and the Rio Grande. Instead, this theory states that the ancestral upper Colorado River flowed from Utah into northern Arizona, then curved back toward southwestern Utah, but its remaining course is unknown. This ancestral river came into existence possibly more than thirty-eight million years ago. Then, about four to five million years ago, the Gulf of California formed and a river emptying into the Gulf began extending its length headward until it captured the ancestral upper Colorado River. The through flowing Colorado River required only two to three million years to cut the Grand Canyon to near its present depth.

Subsequent to the cutting of the canyon, volcanic action in the western portion of the canyon resulted in the formation of several lava dams and associated temporary lakes. The first lava damming occurred about 1,200,000 years ago. Evidence of this activity can be seen in the Toroweap region and remnants of the lava dams are found along the river at Lava Falls. One of the higher lava dams which occurred in the Toroweap area may have stood approximately 1400 feet above the present river level. Another dam in the area of Prospect Canyon is believed to have stood 2300 feet above the river, forming a lake which extended approximately 180 miles to the vicinity of today's Lee's Ferry.

The river cut through the various lava dams and since breaching the last dam has lowered its channel about fifty feet.

The river cuts only its channel. Widening of the canyon has been and is being accomplished by the forces of erosion. Much of the debris resulting from erosion is eventually moved to the river and as it is transported through the canyon it helps to scour the river channel and lower its bed.

The view west at Toroweap
exposes a vista of extensive volcanic activity.
This is one of the regions where the Colorado River
was once dammed by high walls of lava
which streamed into the gorge during more recent and violent
episodes of the geologic history at the Grand Canyon.

THE MOTORIST'S VIEW

SOUTH RIM

The south entrance to Grand Canyon National Park is located two miles north of the small settlement of Tusayan.

From the vicinity of Tusayan to the South Rim the road cuts through a forest of yellow or Ponderosa pine. One and a half miles north of the entrance station the road divides. The road proceeding east from the intersection is known as the East Rim Drive which skirts the South Rim of the canyon to viewpoints along the rim, to Desert View tourist facilities and to Cameron, Arizona where it joins U.S. Highway 89, the most direct automobile route to the North Rim which is only eleven miles across the canyon at Grand Canyon Village, but is 214 miles via the highway.

The road north at the intersection leads to Mather Point, Grand Canyon Village and beyond to the West Rim Drive which continues to western viewpoints on the South Rim and terminates at Hermits Rest.

Mather Point, the first view of the canyon for many visitors, is located less than a mile north on the south entrance road from its intersection with the East Rim Drive. The viewpoint is 6850 feet above sea level and was named for Stephen Tyng Mather, the first director of the National Park Service.

The panorama at Mather Point extends from the Palisades of the Desert, the prominent east wall of the Grand Canyon between the mouth of the little Colorado River and Desert View, westward beyond Bright Angel Creek, the conspicuous southwest trending canyon descending from the north side of the canyon to the Colorado River. The great river is not visible from this viewpoint.

Near the mouth of Bright Angel Creek is Phantom Ranch, a tourist facility accessible on foot, by muleback, or boat. Tourist accommodations at this location were first built in 1903 by David D. Rust and were called Rust's Camp. The name was changed to Roosevelt's Camp in 1913 when Theodore Roosevelt visited the site. Remodeled and enlarged in 1922, the facility was re-named Phantom Ranch because of its proximity to nearby Phantom Creek.

The most prominent landmarks visible from Mather Point are pyramidal Vishnu Temple and massive, flat-topped Wotans Throne, located northeast of the point and eroded out of the north side of the canyon.

Approximately one-half mile northwest of Mather Point is the turn-off to Yavapai Point and Museum, named for the Yavapai Indians. The museum contains geologic exhibits and a formations column built from rocks of the various layers forming the canyon. The rocks have been placed in their proper sequence and orientation.

The Canyon Rim Nature Trail leads along the canyon from Yavapai Museum to the Visitor Center and on to Grand Canyon Village. The Visitor Center museum contains exhibits of the natural and cultural history of the canyon and a display of historic boats used on early river trips through the canyon. The Visitor Center also houses a research library and the offices of the park administration.

Just west of the Visitor Center is the Shrine of the Ages and the Grand Canyon cemetery, the resting place of many canyon pioneers. In the cemetery is a memorial to 128 persons killed in the June 30, 1956 collision of two commercial airliners. The wreckage fell on Chuar Butte near the mouth of the Little Colorado River in the eastern region of the canyon.

Roads opposite the Visitor Center and cemetery lead to the trailer village, campground, picnic area, showers and laundry services, Yavapai Lodge and Restaurant, Babbitt's General Store, the post office and a branch of Valley National Bank.

Grand Canyon Village is three-quarters of a mile west of the Visitor Center and is the location of many of the park's tourist facilities as well as the trailhead for the Bright Angel Trail, one of two main trails from the South Rim into the canyon.

At the eastern end of the village near the rim is Verkamp's souvenir store. The business was founded by John G. Verkamp in 1905, the year the wooden store building was constructed. On display at the store is a large oil painting entitled "Evening-Grand Canyon," which was painted in 1911 by famed artist Louis Aiken.

West of Verkamp's is the Hopi House, a stone building constructed by the Santa Fe Railroad. Though they have been absent for some time, originally, Hopi Indians lived at Hopi House where they worked at their native crafts and performed dances for park visitors.

El Tovar Hotel is located near the Hopi House. The structure is built partially of pine logs and rocks and originally cost $250,000. The hotel opened on January 14, 1905 and was operated by the Fred Harvey Company, a subsidiary of the Santa Fe Railroad. The hotel was named for Pedro El Tovar, an officer in Coronado's army exploring the Southwest in 1540. Although a group of Coronado's men were the first people of European descent to see the Grand Canyon, Pedro de Tovar was not in this group.

When the El Tovar originally opened, it featured roof gardens, a solarium, a music room, a game room, and telephones in all guest rooms. Drinking water was brought by train from a spring 120 miles away. In 1906, rooms were rented on the American Plan, with prices starting at $4.00 per day and the hotel was described as "the most unique, the most comfortable, and one of the costliest resorts in the Southwest."

West of the El Tovar are two contemporary motels, the Kachina Lodge and the Thunderbird Lodge. Beyond these units is the Bright Angel Lodge.

The Bright Angel Lodge was established in 1896 by J. Wilbur Thurber as the Bright Angel Hotel. Later, the Santa Fe Railroad acquired the facility and it was operated as a less expensive alternative to the El Tovar Hotel. The present lodge building was constructed in 1935. The structure was designed by Mary Elizabeth Jane Colter who also designed the nearby curio shop, The Lookout, Hermits Rest, some of the buildings at Phantom Ranch and the Watchtower at Desert View. By the use of native materials and colors, Miss Colter harmonized architecture with the natural environment.

A few hundred feet west of Bright Angel Lodge is the Kolb Studio, at the head of the Bright Angel Trail. The studio was established at the Grand Canyon by Ellsworth and Emery Kolb in 1903, sixteen years before the Grand Canyon was set aside as a national park. The Kolbs were photographers and canyon explorers. The motion picture of their 1911 river expedition through the Grand Canyon has gained the distinction of having played continuously for more years than any other motion picture. Emery Kolb passed away in December, 1976 at the age of 95, having lived at the canyon longer than any other individual and the studio has been closed since his death. The National Park Service owns the building and will convert it for use as a center for interpretation and information.

Mile 147 near Matkatamiba (Manakacha) Canyon.

Next to the Kolb Studio is the head of the Bright Angel Trail. Originally an Indian trail, it was improved in 1890-91 and was operated as a toll trail. Four and a half miles down the trail is Indian Gardens, once a garden spot for the Havasupai Indians. From Indian Gardens, a branch trail crosses the Tonto Platform to the edge of Plateau Point and a view of the Colorado River. From Indian Gardens, the Bright Angel Trial continues to the Kaibab Suspension Bridge, which spans the Colorado, and to Phantom Ranch.

South of the rim's lodges and other facilities are the community building, Park Service buildings, tourist cabins and motel, and cafeteria.

West Rim Drive

West of the Grand Canyon Village, the West Rim Drive follows the canyon's South Rim approximately eight miles through a forest of pinon and juniper to Hermits Rest. The drive provides access to several excellent viewpoints of the canyon. An improved foot trail, the West Rim Trail, parallels the rim of the canyon from the village.

Approximately one mile west of the village on the West Rim Drive is a pull-off which affords a view of the Bright Angel Trail descending the canyon wall to Indian Gardens on the Tonto Platform.

Maricopa Point is two miles from the village. Its elevation is 7050 feet and was named for the Maricopa Indians. Maricopa Point is bounded on the east by Garden Creek Canyon and on the west by the Horn Creek drainage area. From the point, the river cannot be seen, but the Upper Granite Gorge is visible. The gorge is composed of dark, hard schist and gneiss rocks with dikes and sills of pink and white granite. These formations are of Precambrian age and are the oldest exposed rocks in the Grand Canyon. Across the river, Bright Angel Creek Canyon is prominent.

West of Maricopa Point, below the rim, is the site of the Lost Orphan Mine, located by Daniel L. Hogan in 1893. Originally a copper mine, uranium ore was removed from the site in the 1950's.

Beyond Maricopa Point on the West Rim Drive is the Powell Memorial. The memorial was dedicated on May 20, 1918 to honor Major John Wesley Powell and his five man crew for their history making exploration and first water transit of the Grand Canyon in 1869.

Yucca in bloom
along the canyon's dry inner gorge.

The next overlook on the West Rim Drive is at Hopi Point. A memorial to Colonel Claude Hale Birdseye (1878-1941), who led a United States Geological Survey expedition through the canyon in 1923, is located at this point. Hopi Point projects between Horn Creek Canyon on the east and Salt Creek Canyon on the west and, as is possible from most of the overlooks on the rim drive, many of the picturesque buttes and temples on the north side of the canyon can be seen. These include, Vishnu Temple, Wotans Throne, Zoroaster Temple, Brahma Temple, Buddha Temple, Tower of Ra, Cheops Pyramid, Tower of Set, Osiris Temple, Shiva Temple and Isis Temple. Northeast of the point is Dana Butte, named for geologist James Dwight Dana, a noted mineralogist. Hopi Point is named for the Hopi Indians who have had an on-going connection with the Grand Canyon country. The Hopi Indians live about 100 miles east of the Grand Canyon and Hopis of the Third Mesa have made ceremonial treks into the Grand Canyon to gather salt from mines along the east bank of the Colorado River below the mouth of the Little Colorado. The Indians called the special salt *sieunga* and used it in special ceremonies. The salt was also used to flavor food.

The Hopi Trail to the salt mines descended Salt Trail Canyon to the Little Colorado River Canyon and continued approximately seven miles to the Colorado River in the Grand Canyon. Along the trail are several Hopi shrines. The *sipapu*, located four and one half miles from the Colorado on the north bank of the Little Colorado, is, according to Hopi religion, one of the places where man may have emerged into the world. The *sipapu* is a travertine dome, about twenty feet high and ninety feet in diameter. In the top of the dome is a pool of yellowish water approximately ten feet in diameter through which gas bubbles percolate.

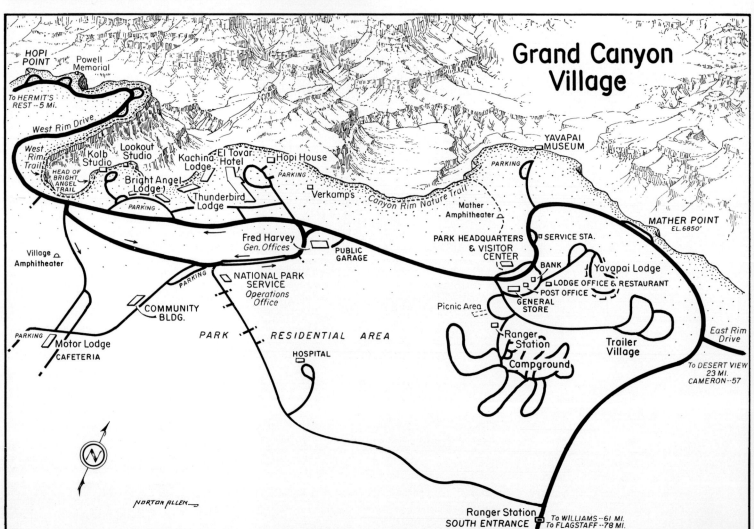

Grand Canyon Village

In the Toroweap region,
the river is crowded to a narrow channel
while canyon walls seem still higher and more rugged.

One mile west of Hopi Point is Mohave Point, named for the Mohave Indians. The Point is between Salt Creek, on the east, and Monument Creek on the west. The upper area of Salt Creek between Mohave Point and Hopi Point is called The Inferno. The ridge extending below Mohave Point between Monument Creek and The Inferno is called the Alligator.

Pima Point, some five miles west of Mohave Point is considered by many to offer the South Rim's finest view of the canyon, possibly because at this point the Colorado River is visible and the view down-canyon is spectacular. Early evening is an excellent time of day to view the canyon from Pima Point as changing light adds many hues to the canyon walls which are not evident in mid-day. Cope Butte lies below the point and two rapids of the Colorado are visible. Four thousand four hundred feet below are Granite Rapid to the east and Boucher Rapid to the west. Here, the river flows through the Upper Granite Gorge consisting of ancient Precambrian formations and above the gorge is the Tonto Platform resting on the vertical walled Tapeats Sandstone. The contact between the dark Precambrian rocks and the overlying brown colored Tapeats Sandstone is called the Great Unconformity, a gap in the geologic record. The Great Uncomformity resulted from a period of extensive erosion before the subsequent deposition of the Tapeats Sandstone.

West of Pima Point, on the Tonto Platform, is the abandoned site of Hermit Camp. From 1912 to 1930, the Fred Harvey Company operated these overnight tourist facilities offering mule trips to the camp and supplying the facility through the use of an aerial tramway which once stretched between Pima Point and the canyon camp. Some evidence of the former camp is distinctly visible from Pima Point. The well constructed Hermit Trail connected the camp with Hermits Rest, now the western terminus of the West Rim Drive.

Hermits Rest, a unique log and stone structure featuring an unusual walk-in fireplace, was built in 1914 and was named for Louis D. Boucher who came to the canyon in 1891 and lived at Dripping Springs, west of Hermits Rest. The white bearded Boucher was not a hermit, although he was known as one because of his isolated camp located in Boucher Canyon where the "hermit" operated a copper mine and small tourist camp.

The East Rim Drive.

The East Rim Drive leaves the south entrance road approximately one and one half miles north of the park entrance station and approximately three miles southeast of Grand Canyon Village. One mile east of the junction, a spur drive leads north to the head of the Kaibab Trail and to Yaki Point Overlook.

The Kaibab Trail is a trans-canyon trail, connecting the North and South Rims. Construction of the trail started in December, 1924 and was completed in September, 1928. The trail is twenty-one miles long and crosses the Colorado River on the Kaibab Suspension Bridge. The bridge is 440 feet long, five feet wide and is approximately sixty-five feet above the river.

Yaki Point (elevation 7250') was named for the Yaki Indians of Mexico. Pipe Creek bounds the point on the west and Cedar Ridge extends below the point to the north. O'Neill Butte is a conspicuous feature below the point, with the Kaibab Trail descending its eastern face. O'Neill Butte was named for William "Bucky" O'Neill who was involved in copper mining in the Grand Canyon. From Yaki Point, views both up and down the canyon are spectacular, with many temples, buttes and spires visible.

The Colorado River and canyon walls below Desert View.

Nearly three miles east of the Yaki Point turnoff is the Duck on a Rock Viewpoint, named for an erosional remnant of Kaibab Limestone which, with imagination, resembles a duck. To the north is the sharp pointed Vishnu Temple with the Palisades of the Desert in view to the east and beyond its cliffs, which form the east wall of the Grand Canyon, is the Painted Desert.

The turn-off to Grandview Point is located five miles east of Duck on the Rock Viewpoint. Grandview Trail begins at the point and leads into the canyon to Horseshoe Mesa some 2400 feet below. Peter D. Berry located a copper mine on Horseshoe Mesa in 1890 and constructed the trail from the point to his mine in 1892 and 1893. As all Grand Canyon trails, the Grandview is strenuous and should not be attempted by anyone not in good physical condition, well-equipped and informed about hiking conditions. This information is available at the Visitor Center in Grand Canyon Village.

A two-story log hotel, the Grandview, was erected near the point in 1895. The hotel was a popular tourist center at the Grand Canyon for a few years, but when the railroad was opened to Grand Canyon Village in 1901, the hotel business declined and eventually the establishment was closed.

Of the many secrets closely guarded by the Grand Canyon,
none is more mysterious or more well kept than the secret of the Anasazi.
Pictured here is the small Nankoweap Ruin located 800 feet above
the Colorado River in a small cave eroded from
the Redwall Limestone of the Marble Gorge. This site was once used by people
who farmed the canyon area during the 12th and 13th centuries,
but who seem to have disappeared from the face of the earth toward the end
of the 13th century. Anthropologists can only speculate
as to the fate of the Anasazi culture and silent ruins scattered
throughout the southwest are but a mute reminder of an expired people.

A boating party quietly passes
beneath towering walls
of Redwall Limestone.

Grandview Point on the South Rim is directly across canyon from the Walhalla Plateau with Cape Royal, one of the North Rim's finest overlooks, at the tip of the plateau. Many of the erosional features carved from the North Rim's geologic strata take an outstanding visual definition when viewed from Grandview Point.

One mile east of Grandview Point, the East Rim Drive descends Buggeln Hill. The hill is part of the Grandview monocline, a structural fold in the earth. The Sinking Ship, a large tilted mass of the monocline, is visible to the northwest from a viewpoint at the bottom of the hill.

The East Rim Drive continues to the short spur road to Moran Point which was named for Thomas Moran, an outstanding 19th Century artist who first visited the canyon at the North Rim in 1873. Moran's paintings of the canyon did much to acquaint the American public with the scenic and natural values of the Grand Canyon.

To the east of Moran Point is Zuni Point and to the west is Coronado Butte.

Tusayan Ruin, one of more than one hundred known Anasazi sites near the South Rim of the Grand Canyon, and Tusayan Museum are located five miles east of Moran Point. The ruin, excavated by Emil Walter Haury in the 1930's, is a pueblo; a communal village, laid out in the shape of the letter "U" with rooms on a plaza. Originally, part of the structure was two stories high and may have contained eight rooms. There were also two round ceremonial rooms known as kivas. On the floor of the kiva was a sipapu, an orifice symbolizing a place through which the ancestors of the Anasazi entered this world. In the center of the kiva's roof was an opening through which light entered and smoke left and also enabled the Indians to climb in and out by ladder. One of the kivas was connected to the pueblo while the other was south of the pueblo's east room.

Tusayan was the Zuni name for the Hopi villages and the South Rim pueblo was named Tusayan even though it was constructed by the Anasazi, the probable ancestors of the Hopi.

Lipan Point, a short distance east of Tusayan Ruin, was originally known as Lincoln Point, but the name was changed in

To visitors who experience the canyon from the rims only, the view is that of an eroding landscape of desert mountains and bottomless fissures through which the Colorado River wends its way. But this is an illusion for deep within the abyss, springs and streams issue from tributary points creating garden spots like Vasey's Paradise which is pictured here.

Majestic Cape Solitude,
at the confluence of the Colorado
and Little Colorado Rivers.

1902 in honor of the Lipan Indians of
Texas. The canyon below Lipan Point is
generally broad, but narrows to the west.
To the northeast, the canyon is cut in soft
sedimentary rocks which are easily eroded;
in the west, the river flows over hard
metamorphic rock of the Upper Granite
Gorge. Unkar Rapid is visible in the broad
canyon area and to the north, up-river, is
the lower end of the Marble Gorge. The
sheer declivity of the Palisades of the
Desert becomes even more profound from
the viewpoint.

At Lipan Point, the Great Unconformity between the Precambrian rocks
and the overlying Paleozoic Sandstone is
visible at the base of the brown verticle
sandstone cliff above the reddish colored
slope leading down to the river in the
broad canyon section and at the top of the
reddish slope leading to the dark Precambrian rock in the narrow Upper Granite
Gorge.

Desert View is the easternmost
designated viewpoint on the East Rim
Drive. The east park entrance station is
located near Desert View and tourist
facilities are provided by Grand Canyon
National Park Lodges.

The Watchtower is a distinctive
architectural feature at Desert View which
can be seen from many South Rim viewpoints and is also visible from the river.
Completed in 1933, the masonry tower is
sixty-seven feet high. At the base, the
diameter is thirty feet and at the top,
twenty-four feet. Inside, a winding
stairway leads to an observation deck at
the summit of the tower. The gift shop, a
large circular room at the base of the
tower represents a kiva, an Indian
ceremonial chamber.

Although many of the canyon's famed
geologic formations, temples, buttes and
side canyons are visible from various viewpoints, each offers a different perspective
of the canyon and South Rim photographic
and sight-seeing possibilities are virtually
limitless.

THE MOTORIST'S VIEW

NORTH RIM

Specific points of interest at the North
Rim include Point Sublime, Cape Royal,
Point Imperial, the North Rim Village,
Bright Angel Point and Toroweap Point.

The North Rim entrance station is
reached via Arizona Highway 67, thirty
miles south of its intersection with U.S.
89A at Jacob Lake; but because North Rim
altitudes vary from 7000 to 9000 feet
above sea level and snowfall in the area
averages 150 inches annually, visitor activity and facilities are limited (depending
upon weather conditions) to a spring to
autumn season.

At the North Rim, October's radiant aspen, brisk winds and cold nights herald the onset of a short autumn season which is soon to be followed by deep snows of winter.

Point Sublime.

One and one-half miles south of the North Rim entrance station, an unpaved side road leads seventeen miles southwest through a spruce-fir and ponderosa pine forest where wild turkeys and mule deer are often seen to Point Sublime at an elevation of 7458 feet. Point Sublime was named by Major Clarence E. Dutton, a member of the USGS party that studied the Grand Canyon in 1880 and 1881. Dutton called the view "the most sublime of the earthly spectacles."

Bright Angel Point, Point Imperial and Cape Royal.

The paved road from the North Rim entrance station proceeds along the edge of a mountain meadow park, and then follows a spruce-fir lined canyon to the summit of Lindbergh Hill, where it passes through a mixed forest of spruce, fir and aspen and then descends to the southern base of the hill, reaching an intersection, eighteen miles south of the entrance station. The road northeast at the junction continues to Point Imperial and Walhalla Plateau viewpoints while the road south ends at the North Rim facilities complex near Bright Angel Point.

Five and one-half miles northeast on the Point Imperial-Walhalla Plateau road, the visitor reaches a Y intersection. The northeast branch road leads to Point Imperial while the southern branch crosses the Walhalla Plateau ending at spectacular Cape Royal.

At an elevation of 8801 feet, Point Imperial is the highest viewpoint in Grand Canyon National Park. The vista extends across the canyon and 3000 feet below to the Marble Platform and the Painted Desert. The prominent spire in the foreground is Mount Hayden, 8350 feet above sea level, named for Charles Trumbull Hayden who, in 1857, founded the city of Tempe, Arizona.

The Walhalla Plateau-Cape Royal road passes small Greenland Lake, two and one-half miles from the Y intersection. The pond is on the west side of the road and in late summer is usually dry. There are few lakes on the Walhalla Plateau because its surface is of Kaibab Limestone. Limestone dissolves in water and as a consequence few lakes form on limestone surfaces. Lakes that do form generally hold water only until the lake bed collapses causing a sinkhole. Greenland Lake is a sinkhole that has become plugged with debris and is again able to support water.

The Vista Encantada viewpoint affords an expansive view of the Painted Desert. Approximately two miles southeast of Vista Encantada are the Anasazi ruins at Walhalla Glades where Indians raised crops during the period from 700 A.D. to 1175 A.D.

Passing through an excellent stand of ponderosa pine, the Walhalla Road continues from Walhalla Glades to Cape Royal. The white-tailed Kaibab squirrel is unique to the ponderosa forest of the Kaibab Plateau. The squirrels nest in the branches of these reddish-barked trees and feed on the pine seeds. A 1932 estimate calculated that there were only one hundred twenty Kaibab squirrels living at the North Rim and many people familiar with the North Rim feel that the Kaibab squirrel population is steadily declining. The squirrels are on the U.S. endangered species list.

Cape Royal, elevation 7876 feet above sea level, at the tip of the Walhalla Plateau, is approximately fourteen and one-half miles south of the Point Imperial-Walhalla junction. A prominent feature at Cape Royal is Angel's Window, a massive arch eroded out of the Kaibab Limestone. One of the short trails which heads at Cape Royal ends directly atop the arch.

Deep within the Marble Gorge,
red stained limestone walls bathed in evening light rise sharply from the banks of the Colorado River.
On August 9, 1869, Powell recorded —
"And now the scenery is on a grand scale. The walls of the canyon, 2,500 feet high, are of marble,
of many beautiful colors, often polished below by the waves, and sometimes far up the sides,
where showers have washed the sands over the cliffs. At one place I have a walk
for more than a mile on a marble pavement, all polished and fretted with strange devices
and embossed in a thousand fantastic patterns. Through a cleft
in the wall the sun shines on this pavement and it gleams in iridescent beauty."

Twisting and turning in their tortuous course,
canyon walls are in constant change from sunlit brilliance to menacing shadow.

From Cape Royal, the intermediate, nearly level Tonto Platform can be seen. To the east is Freya Castle, and to the south are Rama Shrine, Vishnu Temple and Coronado Butte. The massive flat-topped temple to the south is Wotans Throne. On clear days, the lofty volcanic peaks of the San Francisco Mountains may be seen in the distant south. The mountains are situated just north of Flagstaff, Arizona with the highest summit, Humphrey's Peak, attaining an altitude of 12,633 feet above sea level. West of Cape Royal are the Angel's Gate, Zoroaster Temple, Isis Temple, Brahma Temple, Shiva Temple and Deva Temple.

Bright Angel Point is located south of the intersection of the park's north entrance station and the Point Imperial-Cape Royal roads. The parking lot at the northern head of the trans-canyon Kaibab Trail is situated one mile south of the intersection on the road to Bright Angel Point. Opposite the Kaibab Trail parking lot, an unpaved road descends to a meadow and a parking area for the Widforss Point Trail, named for Gunnar Mauritz Widforss, noted watercolor artist of the Grand Canyon.

One mile beyond the Kaibab Trail parking area are the North Rim Village tourist facilities which include a service station, general store, campground and a park ranger station. Grand Canyon Lodge is located a little more than a mile from the village area. This beautiful rock and timber structure was completed in 1928, but the interior burned in a 1932 fire and reconstruction of the lodge was not concluded for several years.

The lodge is situated near the end of Bright Angel Point. The Bright Angel Nature Trail follows the canyon rim along the point. Below the point is Bright Angel Canyon and to the east are the weathered battlements of Deva Temple, Brahma Temple and Zoroaster Temple.

Rapids of Havasu Creek.

The wild burros of the Grand Canyon
were once used as beasts of burden
by prospectors and miners,
but as their owners suspended their search
for wealth and the burros were
no longer needed, the animals
were often turned loose
in the canyon giving rise to
a wild burro population.

The Colorado River and south wall of the Grand Canyon at Mile 107.

Toroweap.

Toroweap Point, which offers spectacular views of western portions of the canyon not seen from other developed areas of either the North or South Rims was part of Grand Canyon National Monument until 1975 when the monument was merged with the National Park.

The point is on the North Rim of the canyon and vehicular access to the area is over a sixty mile unpaved road which begins at a turn-off approximately five miles west of Fredonia, Arizona. The turn-off is reached via either Arizona Highway 389 from the east or Utah Highway 59 from the west.

Five miles north of the canyon rim at Toroweap is the Tuweap Ranger Station and campground, but no other visitor facilities are located in the area. In most seasons, no water is available.

At the rim, the overlook affords magnificent views of the deep, narrow canyon and the Colorado River, 2802 feet below. In this area, displays of past volcanic activity are in abundant evidence. Lava flows cover the Esplanade, a conspicuous inner canyon platform in the western Grand Canyon. The Esplanade formed where the easily eroded Hermit Shale was removed above the hard Supai Sandstone. Vulcan's Throne, a cinder cone, is situated on the brink of the canyon. The cone is about three-quarters of a mile in diameter and 567 feet high.

During periods of past volcanic activity, lava flows cascaded over the rim of the canyon and oozed into the Colorado River. On his historic 1869 river voyage, Major John Wesley Powell observed the lava coated canyon walls. Reflecting on the occurrence of the lava cascading into the river, he wrote "What a conflict of water and fire there must have been here! Just imagine a river of molten rock running down into a river of melted snow. What a seething and boiling of the waters; what clouds of steam rolled into the heavens!"

Far below, in the Colorado, Vulcan's Forge projects approximately fifty feet out of the water. Also called Lava Pinnacle, Vulcan's Forge is a volcanic neck, the hard remnant core of a small volcano which once formed in the river.

Lava Falls, the most treacherous and rated the most severe of the Colorado River's rapids, is visible down river from the rim overlook. The falls, also known as Vulcan Rapid, has a thirty-seven foot drop. The rapid is approached by boaters with both anticipation of the thrilling run and apprehension of the inherent dangers. Lava Falls is located 180 miles down-river from the head of the Grand Canyon near Lee's Ferry and 98 miles up-river from the terminus of the canyon at the Grand Wash Cliffs.

The fossil of a Nautiloid,
distant ancestor to the octopus,
is exposed in an eroded stream
channel in Nautiloid Canyon.

Pages 116-117,
the Marble Platform,
Chuar Butte and the Palisades of the Desert.

The western portion of the canyon has seen recent events of geologic violence.
Lava flows seen streaming around desert peaks once poured over the canyon rims
and flowed to the river, blocking its passage.
Upon seeing similar black cascades, Powell wrote:
"From this volcano vast floods of lava have been poured down into the river,
and a stream of molten rock has run up the canyon three or four miles and down
we know not how far. The whole north side as far as we can see is lined with the black basalt,
and high up on the opposite wall are patches of the same material,
resting on the benches and filling old alcoves and caves, giving the wall a spotted appearance."
Powell continued: "What a conflict of water and fire there must have been here!
Just imagine a river of molten rock running down into a river of melted snow.
What a seething and boiling of waters; what clouds of steam rolled into the heavens!"

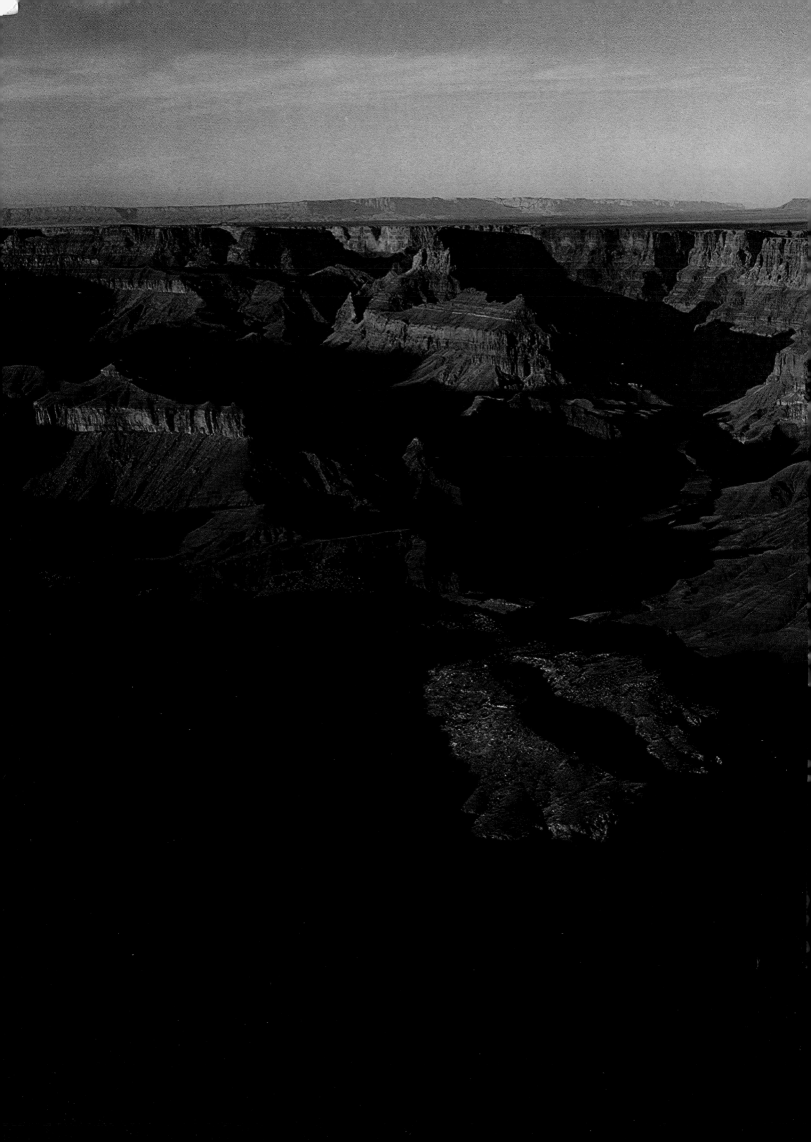

A tiny barrel cactus
colorfully proclaims that spring
has come to the North Rim.

ACKNOWLEDGMENTS
The publisher and staff wish to express their gratitude to the following:

For reviewing the text of this publication.
Merle E. Stitt, Superintendent, Grand Canyon National Park, and Park Rangers assigned to the Division of Interpretation: Robert Butterfield, William Clark, Timothy Manns, and John O'Brien.

Raft and aerial transportation for Mr. Yandell's photographic expeditions secured from Grand Canyon Expeditions, Kanab, Utah.

Black and white reproductions of historical pictures, pages 26, 27, 37, 45, 53, 56 and 93 purchased from Henry E. Huntington Library and Art Gallery, San Marino, California.

Mr. Hoffman wishes to acknowledge the assistance of the following firms and individuals who were instrumental in the preparation of the text: Arizona Historical Society, Grand Canyon National Park Research Library, Museum of Northern Arizona, San Diego Public Library, William G. Bass, George H. Billingsley, Arthur S. Gallenson, Louise M. Hinchliffe, Dr. and Mrs. Ralph L. Hoffman, Emery C. Kolb, Ernest V. Kolb, P. T. Reilly, John H. Riffey, Marc S. Smith, Mr. and Mrs. Ronald R. Smith.

From the South Rim's Kaibab Trail.